UNDER THE TABACHÍN TREE

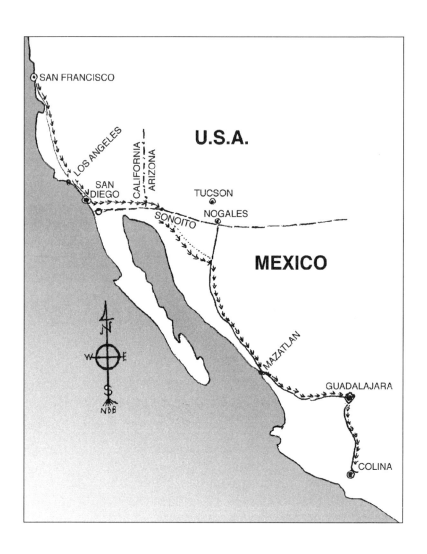

Under The Tabachín Tree

✧ ✧ ✧

A New Home in Mexico

by

Celia Wakefield

Illustrations by Naomi Boulton

Celia Wakefield

CREATIVE ARTS BOOK COMPANY
Berkeley • California 1997

Under the Tabachín Tree is published by Donald S. Ellis
and distributed by Creative Arts Book Company.

For information contact:
Creative Arts Book Company
833 Bancroft Way
Berkeley, California 94710

ISBN 0-88739-121-4
Library of Congress Catalog Number 96-71032

Printed in the United States of America

Cover art and illustrations by Naomi Boulton

Table of Contents

Acknowledgements

During my years in Mexico, many people have helped me with advice and encouragement. I wish, especially, to thank Larry and Betty Waldron for their editorial assistance and Naomi Boulton for her illustrations.

UNDER THE TABACHÍN TREE

Prologue

It was my first evening at the boardinghouse in Mexico City some years ago. The menu included *frijolitos* (little beans) accompanied by *tortillitas* (small tortillas). The meal was served by a maid named Esperancita (Little Hope). However, everything was of normal size. When I heard Manuelito, one of the other boarders, ask for a drink of water, *"por favorcito"* (little please), I became aware that there is a philosophy inherent in Mexican-style Spanish: a view of life through the small end of opera glasses. The opposite of Alice in Wonderland, Mexicans have eaten of a plant which reduces, not themselves, but everything around them.

This, to one fresh out of a country where perspectives are large — the fastest freeways, tallest redwood trees, biggest hamburgers — was a surprise. I decided to look into the difference in more detail.

Reduction, I found, is applied equally to immeasurable ideas and measurable objects. In my daily wanderings around Mexico City I encountered the diminutive. On the main street loomed an enormous equestrian statue, a monument that was a landmark for blocks around. This was invariably referred to as the *Caballito* (Little Horse).

One day as I was waiting in the doctor's office a Mexican woman came in, her hulking son in tow writhing in pain. His mother gave the familiar wave of the hand, the slight shrug.

"Is the doctor busy?" she asked the nurse. "My small son has a slight pain in his little stomach."

But the most useful minimizing word in the language is an intangible one: *ahorita* (little now). *Ahora* means "now." Shall we go home now? *Ahorita*. Is dinner ready? *Ahorita*.

It's the biggest mental obstacle a North American must jump in order to live happily in Mexico.

At first there seems something treacherous and dishonest about "little now." Is it now or isn't it? It isn't now, of course, but it could be sometime soon. After a few weeks in Mexico (unless you have already retreated to the tallest skyscrapers, the widest cornfields, or the state with the greatest number of mountains over 14,000 feet high) you find yourself saying *ahorita* frequently. You feel a sense of relaxation and peace with this word; you have taken the present and future into your confidence. Also, whoever was bothering you about getting things done has stopped. *Ahorita* is an unanswerable word.

I was surprised to find that variations on this theme are possible. "Little now" can become smaller - *ahoritita*. This word was used by a dressmaker to whom I had gone to pick up a positively promised skirt. On advice from an experienced native I waited two weeks before haunting her again.

Ahorititita (little little little now) I encountered at a hotel in Acapulco, a city where such a word is as suitable as languorous palm trees and rum laced with coconut milk.

It was one of those small tragedies which occur in a hastily modernized country. The water faucet disintegrated in my hand, leaving the plumbing system, as the Mexicans put it, "entirely dis-composed." Fleeing from a mounting torrent I yelled for the desk clerk. He turned the water off with a wrench. The faucet, he told me, would be fixed *ahorititita*.

That is to say, today is a holiday and no one works, tomorrow is Saturday, plumbers are off call...Sunday, well that's Sunday. On Wednesday, although the repair would be done in the instant future, I moved to a hotel where there was normal running water.

Why was the clerk so optimistic? *Ahorititita* sounds like the nearest now there is. But it turns out to be never. I started to suspect that the more diminutive endings there are on this simple word, the more remote it becomes.

The implications of my discovery bowled me over. "When will now be now and how can it be never?" I would find myself muttering, or "Is never ever now and when will it be then?"

At this point my visa ran out, not *ahorita* but now, and I returned to the U.S. The jolt of the landing plane was matched by a mental jolt as I returned to my native country, where now is strictly now and never isn't lurking around every corner. I found I was no longer acclimated to the efficiency of timetables and cafeteria host-esses. I quailed at the speedy service in stores where I was waited on immediately without delay or badinage.

After I had been home a while I settled down. I got used again to the point of view where nothing is worthy of much pride unless, like a ripe olive, it is mammoth or colossal. The importance of time again loomed properly large, especially when applied to schedules or deadlines. But I think my subconscious was permanently affect-ed because every once in a while, even years later, I would find myself mumuring, "Why must now be now and when can it be never?"

The Beginning

We reached a turning point in our lives: time for Bill to retire. We had no children and there were just the two of us, plus Sam the dog, to consider. We decided to try a new environment in Mexico, where we had spent many vacations, and chose Colima, a semi-tropical city of medium size. It lies thirty-five miles inland from Pacific beaches, and a half day's drive in the other direction from the metropolis of Guadalajara. Guide books give Colima little space although we knew, from driving through it, that it is a beautiful white city at the foot of a steaming volcano. We felt like going there if only to see why it was ignored.

Our last night in Berkeley Bill and I were restless. We had sold all our furniture except a bed, and Sam clattered over bare floors and stared out uncurtained windows. We would start south at dawn.

Lying there in the dark, I thought that this was the first exciting step into a new life. It felt dangerous. What if we were starting on something that would not work out at all? Were we young enough, resilient enough to adjust or would we give up, come home and do something else? The second option, I realized uneasily, was only academic. We could hardly afford financially, after making such a drastic change, to start over. Maybe we couldn't afford it mentally either. I finally fell asleep and in a moment it was five o'clock, time to go.

The house was empty but the VW camper was full. The bottom layer of cargo included TV, record player, pictures, books, Japanese screen, mango coffee table from Hawaii, things we didn't want to part with. Then came clothes, pots and pans, sheets and towels. On top of all Sam, the German pointer, sat enthroned. Along with him went his big water bucket, slopping over occasionally to dampen whatever was near it.

As we drove south on the Nimitz Highway the sun came up. San Francisco emerged from the dark a white wonder city, and the Golden Gate a glittering red-gold span. Gulls hovered over the bay where an early morning breeze raised only ripples. Fog hung over the hills of Marin County across the water. Overhead a jet roared off in the direction of Reno.

Berkeley was a fine place to live, I thought. During the last quarter century all sorts of interesting things had happened to us here, some good, some bad...all now over forever.

Better not think of that, I told myself, think only of the future. It's going to be interesting, good or bad, that's for sure.

"Of course we're coming back here in six months to pick up the rest of our things," Bill said somberly. He is from the state of Washington where speech is deliberate. His drawl made the words sound very sad.

"Forget it," I said. "Think how we used to look forward to Mexican vacations. That's what this is going to be...a really good, extended vacation, doing just what we want to do whenever we want to do it. Soon Colima will feel like home."

I spoke cheerfully to hide my apprehension. Bill, his tall frame crouched over the wheel, said nothing more. Sam whined softly behind us. In my mind I ran over the points we had so often discussed. Mexican retirement. Its advantages: less expensive living, a fine climate, friendly people, our experience of many happy trips below the border and our fair knowledge of Spanish, an opportunity to relax far from the stresses at home. Its disadvantages: leaving friends behind, starting over at retirement age, always to be a foreigner in a strange land. I thought the benefits came out ahead, Bill had doubts. We had agreed to give it a good long trial before calling the change permanent.

"I hope it will be our home," Bill said. "We'll see in a couple of years."

We turned inland. The Bay, with its shiny rippling waves, was lost to view. A solitary seagull hovered over us for a while, then wheeled back towards the ocean.

In and Out of Sonoyta

"Here we are in sunny Mexico." Bill swerved around a heap of broken bottles to park the combi in a strip of shade by Sonoyta's customs shed. "Berkeley seems a long way off. Wonder what they're doing up there."

We had crossed the border from Arizona and had been directed to this desert spot for immigration and customs routine.

"I couldn't care less what they're doing in Berkeley," I said.

I glanced at Bill as he opened his door. He looked sweaty, tired, discouraged. His hair, nowadays more gray than blond, lay plastered to his head. He stopped by the car and took off his glasses to wipe them. I felt the surge of affection which a quarter century of his company had not diminished.

"Yesterday it was sunny Gila Bend," he remarked. "One hundred and ten in the shade. I saw a thermometer at the motel. Here it's got to be a hundred and twenty."

Sam sprawled on the heap of luggage, lapping thirstily at his water bowl. We had kept him comfortable in the August heat by laying towels soaked in ice water across his back but I didn't see any source of ice around here. The customs shed sat alone by Highway 2, a minor road leading eventually to the main West Coast Highway 15. Scanning the immense cactus-covered desert around us I remembered a mural in a Guadalajara cafe: a thirst-parched man eternally crawling through miles of sand toward a cool bottle of Cuervo tequila.

We were the only travelers in sight. A cock crowed proudly in the distance. Flies buzzed in and out of a broken window in the customs building. A heavy smell of bananas pervaded the combi. I fumbled in the glove compartment and handed our folder of papers to Bill. We had tourist visas, American passports, car registration. And, oh yes, Sam's papers: the vet's report of a physical exam, innoculation certificates with stamps affixed to them in Sacramento and the flourishing signature of the Mexican consul in San Francisco.

"If they search the combi we may not get into Mexico," I said as I jumped out of the car, "but Sam can surely make it with all his papers." I had a quick mental picture of a German pointer, his documents in a handy shoulder bag, hitchhiking down the Pacific coast thirteen hundred miles to Colima.

No sign of anyone around. I glanced up at the blue sky, empty except for a few vultures circling. In this desert the man in the Guadalajara mural would never make it to the tequila.

I thought guiltily of things in the car, not the innocuous dishes, sacks of dog food, suitcases, but what lay beneath: color TV, stereo, radio, electric oven, steam iron, tape recorder — all the comforts we were importing for our Mexican home. This was long before any free trade agreement. Our things weren't new, perhaps they were not forbidden, but why take a chance by declaring them.

I felt unprotected at this lonely roadside post. Anything could happen here. If our possessions were frowned on by an irate inspector, there would be a big fine. He might even confiscate them.

"Have you got the *mordida* money ready?" Bill asked, as we sidestepped a pile of old newspapers and reached the office door. Bill still has a touching faith in my powers of persuasion through womanly wiles, and had elected me to do the persuading.

"I don't think we will have to pay a bribe," I said bravely, feeling in my pocket for the U.S. currency to be dispensed if necessary.

"What makes you think that?"

"Just a feeling."

Bill snorted. "Well, I don't have that feeling. I'll nod when it's time to hand over the money."

"All right," I said, thinking that years ago money might not have been needed. Now I am no longer of an age when I can hope to improve a situation with a charming smile or a burst of girlish tears. When the screen door slammed behind us and I saw the customs officer's face I realized that youth and smiles would not affect him. Yet for some reason I felt optimistic. Maybe the heat and dust had unsettled my brain. I thought of Sam waiting in the car and hoped he wasn't suffocating.

The inspector was alone in the shack, but there were signs that others had been there: two extra desks littered with papers, a chair pushed back from one with a big sombrero lying on it. I guessed the assistants were out for a refreshing beer.

"I'll bet you all the money in my pocket that we don't have to pay," I muttered to Bill, easing myself onto a pink plastic chair with a bent leg.

"It's a bet." Bill smiled. He settled his thin six-foot frame on a high wooden stool which made him look even taller than usual. His expression reminded me that I never win bets. The customs officer straightened up, his shoulders just a little above the desk, and glared at Bill looming above him. Bill smiled and nodded in a friendly way.

The inspector wore a pair of brown riding pants with puttees, a red checked shirt with a black tie slightly askew, and a gray military jacket with one epaulet. His short black hair bristled fiercely. His glasses reflected the outdoor sunlight in little sharp flashes. He rolled an unlit cigar slowly from side to side in his mouth. Sixty years old, maybe? Forty long years on the job in the Sonora desert?

"*No hablo inglés.*" He frowned over a huge ledger. With a placating smile Bill leaned forward to offer his folder of papers. The inspector waved it aside.

"*Momentito.*" He chomped on his cigar as he flipped another page of his ledger. "*Momentito. Estoy muy ocupado.*"

He stared at the paper and continued to ignore us. Occasionally he took the cigar from his mouth, scowled at the tip as though wondering why it wasn't lighted, then reinserted it. I was very hot and eager to get going. I was wearing shorts. My sweaty legs stuck to the pink plastic seat. I wondered if I might leave with a chair stuck to my behind. Bill shifted uneasily on his stool. The dust-encrusted wall clock showed 12:25, full heat of the day. A fly walked over the figure 12 very slowly.

"*No tenemos nada de importancia, Señor,*" I said sweetly. "Not a thing of importance in the car. My husband has all the papers right here. We know you are very busy and this just requires a little signature perhaps."

The officer turned a page and shifted the cigar from left to right in his mouth.

I studied the ceiling where spider webs covered the corners. Up there a large fat spider sat absolutely still. A small insect ambled innocently toward the web... The spider waited... The insect approached. Suddenly the customs officer banged a paper weight on the desk.

"*Documentos!*" he barked. Bill was dozing. "*Documentos! En seguida!*"

Bill jumped and in his haste to obey dropped the file. Papers and passports scattered among cigar stubs and chiclet wrappers on the floor. Bill gathered the documents together and laid them on the desk. The inspector drew himself up as tall as possible and balanced his cigar on the ashtray.

"*Firma aquí...otra firma aquí!*" He shouted for signatures like a sergeant marshaling combat troops. I unstuck myself from my chair to sign where necessary. He studied our passport pictures with disdain. Then he slapped the passports shut.

"*Su perrito,*" he growled. "Where is that *animal?*"

"*Sí,* of course, our dog," Bill said. "In car. Papers here. Dog papers."

The inspector studied them.

"You name a dog Sam...Cocoa...von Lightner!" He raised his eyes to the ceiling. "I don't believe it. *No es posible.* Your car, where is it?"

He was at the door, motioning us through. We followed meekly along to the car. Bill stooped more than usual to make the inspector look taller.

There is room for everything in a VW camper, and we had everything in ours, but I did not see Sam. The doors were locked, the windows open but protected by screens. The dog could not have gotten out. The sun, however, had moved while we were indoors. Wherever he was, Sam was uncomfortable. Then I saw a stub of tail sticking up between two sacks of towels and blankets. The inspector didn't notice. He had bent down to peer beneath the chassis.

"Arms...pistols...guns tied below sometimes. *Contrabanda.*" He stalked slowly around staring in the car windows. "Washing machines ... refrigerators ... electric knives and blenders...*Contrabanda!*" He repeated his litany but what he saw was a beach umbrella, a garden chair, one rubber boot, a sleeping bag, six rolls of toilet paper, a jumble of loose magazines and books. We had packed neatly but the roads were rough and cargo had shifted.

"Underneath you have a television!" The inspector turned abruptly to face us. "I do not see it, but I know it. It is in color. You have a radio, a tape recorder. *Qué más, quién sabe!*" He stamped his foot; the metal cleats on his boot rang on the cement of the parking lot. "You Gringos are all alike...*Todos contrabandistas...Todos!*"

Bill gave the signal for a bribe. He pointed, none too subtly, at my pocket, but I pretended not to notice.

"Open the door, remove everything at once...*en seguida!*" The sun flashed on the inspector's glasses. He raised his hand in a dramatic gesture. "Everything out!"

Bill nodded to me again. He anxiously patted his own pocket and pointed at mine. A familiar expression crossed his face. It said, "Don't be an imbecile, Celia!"

Surely this was the *mordida* moment, but I shook my head slightly. For once, I wanted to win a bet.

Bill gave me a look that rivaled the inspector's for fierceness. "Please," he said. I waited, nervously watching the vultures circling in a clear sky.

"EVERYTHING OUT! EVERYTHING!"

I unlocked the middle door of the van. I could see Sam's stub of tail moving slowly back and forth. It stopped. A spotted rear end emerged from between the sacks, made a sharp turn, and was replaced by the forequarters and head of a large hound.

"*Dónde está su perro?* Where is that animal?"

The inspector had not mastered Sam's description on the forms. He expected a tiny beast, a miniature Chihuahua, perhaps, not a seventy-pound hunting dog.

"*Su perrito.* The little dog who is called with a stupid name."

Sam rose suddenly to his full height on top of the baggage. He glared down at the inspector and growled menacingly.

"This is Sam Cocoa von Lightner," I said. "*Es perro bravo...de veras feroz.* Ferocious dog. Stays always in the car. You wish to enter?"

Sam growled again, louder. His hackles rose. His lips curled, framing long fangs. The inspector jumped back and slammed himself against the customs shed. Sam lunged toward the car door, which I quickly closed.

"If you wish," I told the inspector, "we will ourselves affix the customs seal, since I believe it must go on the inside of the windshield. You do not need to enter, Señor."

"Sí...sí," the officer mumbled, handing over a seal for the windshield and another for the rear window. Then, adjusting his glasses, he became stern again. He passed us our tourist visas, stamped for entry into Mexico.

"You have wasted my time," he shouted, as we got back into the car. "I who am always *muy ocupado.* Why did you not say that you had nothing of value?"

It was my turn to drive. Bill quickly pasted on the customs labels while I started the engine.

"That is a very stupid name for a dog," the inspector called after us. "Pass along at once!"

We passed, just as an American sports car with two young men in it parked by the building. Looking in the rear view mirror I saw the inspector bending menacingly over the car while the tourists opened the trunk, unloading everything...everything.

Bill let out a sigh. I smiled. "All right," he said, laughing and patting my shoulder. "This time you win. I'll treat you to a shrimp dinner in Guaymas."

On the Way

We were seven days on the 2300 mile trip from Berkeley to Colima. Beaches, mountains, fields, parched desert plains, rivers and lagoons. We crowded around buses and trucks when an opening in the traffic appeared, chugged up curving mountain roads, the VW laboring under its load. We took rest stops at rubbish-littered Pemex gas stations.

From the customs shed in Sonoyta to Guaymas the highway passed through miles and miles of dry country with nothing to be seen but scruffy little towns and the large modern city of Hermosillo. At Guaymas we reached the ocean, following a natural curve of bay. We still felt close, too close, to the barren hills lying just inland.

Navojoa, Los Mochis, Guasave, Culiacán — towns and cities slipped one by one behind us. Now we drove through marshy lagoon-filled country where white herons thronged, where sluggish rivers emptied their muddy contents in the sea. The smell of swampland mingled with the salty tang of ocean. I thought of mangroves, palm-thatched huts and crocodiles. Always inland rose high mountains, hazy slate-blue in the distance.

At last the port of Mazatlán, a coastal fisherman's resort. We took a day off there to rest, swim, and gather courage for the miles ahead. Sam trotted back and forth on the beach, sniffing for crabs.

Mazatlán, on the ocean, to Tepíc in the mountains was a hard day's trip for us. West Coast Highway 15 was a two-lane paved road. Buses, trucks and cars barreled around curves and hurtled down grades, only then to inch up hill. Occasionally the flow of traffic stopped as cattle crossed. Cargo trucks hurried to and from the U.S. border; up with tomatoes, onions, frozen shrimp; back with manufactured goods. Looking up at the rugged peaks on our left I thought of the poppy kings up there raising their crops for the surreptitious shipment of "goma" to their United States drug contacts.

Now we left the ocean and climbed into mountains, rising curve after tortuous curve to Tepíc, 5000 feet above the sea. After a night in Tepíc, an austere, cold place, we were on our way through more mountains towards the bustling city of Guadalajara. Again, for us it was a whole day's run and the sun was setting as we crossed the highway which girdles Mexico's second largest city. I could see smoke from factory chimneys, hear the drone of planes over the airport, feel the gathering tension of a couple of million people doing all sorts of things.

On this last night of the trip, although we found a comfortable motel where even Sam was welcome, we were restless. We were nearing the end of our journey, with only four more hours of driving to reach Colima. We didn't know where we would stay there or what our welcome would be. We had tried to prepare for our arrival in the city by placing an advertisement in the newspaper *Diario de Colima* asking to rent a house or apartment. We received no answers.

We had heard that the only good motel in Colima would not take pets. With Sam along that was out. We had also heard of another motel in Colima. It was reported to be a busy whorehouse with tenants changing hourly. Dogs welcome, however.

"This whole thing may be a lousy idea," Bill said, as he mixed us a drink that evening in Guadalajara. "The best thing about Mexico this trip is the liquor. The rum's excellent. I'd forgotten about that. We can add it to our 'good' list."

"We decided to retire to Mexico," I said smugly, "to seek 'new horizons' as I believe you called them. What's the matter with Guadalajara for a new horizon?"

"We're not going to stay here," Bill pointed out. His scowl turned into a smile, for he really is a sweet-natured person. "You can be the one to find our Colima house," he said, "and furniture and maid (that's one of the 'good' things on the list, isn't it?) while I'll be out playing golf."

"All right," I said, "I think it'll all be fun — well, not all maybe but enough."

"I got some sleep last night," Bill said at breakfast, "and I feel better, although we may still be wrong. I could have stayed in Berkeley and practiced medicine part time, got a job in a clinic..."

"Now here we are with what remains of our possessions," I said. "Let's stick it out for a while anyway...at least until we get where we're going."

"It's mostly that we're tired from the long drive. Cheer up, honey." Bill flashed me a smile. He closed the overnight bag and opened the door to where the combi waited in front. "Perhaps we should have retired to Cuernavaca or San Miguel de Allende where there are lots of foreigners and people like us are expected."

"We didn't want to do that. 'Adventure' is what we said. 'Let's get away from all the other Americans.' That's what we said."

Sam, saying nothing, leaped into the car and took his usual place on top of the heap.

"At least the dog is having fun," I said.

"And he doesn't try to get in the last word either, you notice," Bill remarked.

Leaving Guadalajara we passed all the sights of a big city: cement plants, railroad station, dignified mansions and sloppy shanties, tree-lined boulevards and jasmine-covered cottages. Bill showed splendid aplomb as he guided the combi through the early morning traffic. A roller coaster has nothing on the busier streets of Guad, as some Americans call it.

We stopped for lunch at Ciudad Guzmán, still in the central plateau country, and shortly afterwards the Colima volcano came into view. We started our tortuous descent toward the ocean. Guadalajara is more than 5,000 feet in elevation, Colima a mere 1500. It seemed that we made that descent many times. The winding two-lane highway was dotted with trucks and buses, all driven by hyperthyroid madmen. *Barrancas* - huge ravines - separated rugged pineclad mountains from green valleys with corn fields in them. Very few towns but quite a supply of roadside crosses. A really religious people, I thought, to put up shrines in such unlikely spots. Sometimes it was a simple wooden cross or heap of pebbles with a cross on top, sometimes an elaborate niche in the rocky hillside with a gaudy religious statue and bunches of plastic flowers. Later we learned that every marker meant a driver who hadn't made it, and the elaborate grottoes sometimes memorialized a whole group of victims.

There were few houses visible although we could see corn fields and rows of spiky maguey cactus set out along almost vertical hillsides. In one deep ravine, on a river, we saw and smelled the sulphurous paper manufacturing town of Atenquique, a model company town it seemed, neat and pretty, a good place to live if the residents could hold their noses all day long.

"We're almost into Colima," Bill said, as we swooped around a curve and saw white buildings, streets, and churches clustered below us. "What if we can't find a decent motel? We'll have to sleep in the car with all the baggage."

"What's that," I said, as we came to the edge of town. "Take a look."

MOTEL LOS CANDILES, OPENING AUGUST 25TH. Mexico frowns on roadside signs advertising hotels miles ahead of time. We were already starting down the palm-shaded main boulevard of town. August 25th and this was August 27th. Not only a place to stay but a pretty place, freshly landscaped, built in Mexican style of brick and plaster with a red tile roof.

"Perhaps we didn't need to worry." Bill parked in the motel driveway. "But we'll have to talk them into taking the dog. You do it. You were great at the border. No bets this time."

I apprehensively scouted for a dog lover. The girl at the desk made a thoughtful face. *"Un perro chico, un perro grande?"* She had evidently not yet been briefed on the subject of pets, and the new place needed tenants. She smiled and put her finger to her nose, considering. Then she nodded. We moved in fast, before she could change her mind. Sam, to be certain of possession, raised his leg and peed on the door to our room.

Thus began a pleasant friendship with the pretty girl Mina, and her bosses, Berto and Titi Reyes. True to the hospitable nature of Colima, which we later came to know, they gave us every care. They directed us to stores, recommended a bank, took phone messages, offered advice on any subject. The cook in the motel restaurant was deeply immersed in a copy of Julia Child's Mastering the Art of French Cooking, in Spanish, which she kept on the counter by her stove. She hadn't got far, I think. I don't remember Julia dwelling on the delights of tacos and enchiladas.

Room 71

Our room at *Los Candiles* overflowed with the contents of the VW and with Sam and with Bill and me. We suffered from the inevitable tourist trouble of the first few days, plus heat, plus mosquitoes, plus a sad feeling of having been rudely uprooted from our familiar round and pushed into a strange, disagreeable layer of time. We stopped discussing who had planned this trip, because we were too deeply into it.

"I've had it with the motel," Bill said one morning. "Let's get on with finding ourselves a home."

"All right," I told him. "It's a couple of days since Berto put that ad in the *Diario de Colima* for us. We ought to be hearing of some places to rent, I should think."

For ten days now we had shared one small room with our record player, television, books, clothes, frying pans, camp stove, sheets and blankets, sacks of dog food, dog's water bucket, and the dog that went with it. All these things we expected to need in our new Mexican home. What home?

We had already learned that Colima had no furnished houses for rent. We would have to take an empty house and start from scratch. We had two answers to our newspaper ad.

We were driven to the first house by its owner, Señor Palacio, in his Mercedes.

"This place looks as though Maximilian and Carlota had just moved out," Bill muttered, as we prowled through the high-ceilinged rooms. There were four bedrooms, six bathrooms. Later we puzzled over this. What would we do with six bathrooms? How many could we use at once? Should we run around flushing just to hear the noise?

The walls were painted in tender colors of mauve, rose and baby-lizard green. Several baroque chandeliers decorated the living and bedrooms. Later we heard the story of the lighting system, remembered from thirty years before. Señor Palacio's father had built his huge house sparing nothing on ostentation, especially on the chandeliers, which were reputed to be embedded in gold bases. Came the night of the grand housewarming with relatives and guests crowding in from Guadalajara and Mexico City. The lights were turned on and out of the crystal chandeliers flowed a fine stream of hot water.

"We'll think it over," Bill told Sr. Palacio, as we made our escape.

"Sam would love it," I said, when the dog met us at our motel room. "He's a natural aristocrat as you know."

"Well, we aren't," Bill said. "It didn't look like a retirement cottage exactly."

Berto described the other possible home, a beautiful historic place dating from Colima's early years four centuries ago. It had sixteen bedrooms and one bathroom. We declined it sight unseen. Certainly we were hard to please.

The next day we learned that part of a new section of the city was now built up and ready. After a ride of inspection with Manuel Gomez, owner of several new houses, we agreed to rent one.

"I must tell you," he said, "that there is no electricity as yet. Otherwise your house is complete. The street, as you can see" — he stepped over a large open ditch — "is nice and new. In four or five days light poles will be in. Meantime, until you have electricity, the house is rent-free."

"That is," he added, the blue eyes inherited from his Irish

grandmother twinkling, "we hope for lights in four or five days. It could be a little longer."

"This is Mexico," I muttered to Bill. "I bet it will be a couple of weeks."

We all joined in the laughter.

The house, one of four on a short street, was modern, clean, freshly painted, with a view of the volcano. A few days with candles would still be better than our cramped existence at the motel. We moved in, saying good-bye-to Mina, Berto, Titi, and Julia's kitchen disciple.

Colima had been making its first impression on us and of course we had already made an impression on Colima. Whatever the motel people may have thought of us, they remembered, during the following two years, the exact room we had had. Whenever we booked quarters for visiting friends the girl at the desk (no longer pretty Mina) always inquired, "Would you like your visitors to have the same room you had when you came to Colima? It was Number 71."

Some day they ought to put a brass plaque on the door saying, "The Wakefields Slept Here."

*****

"At least we have a home now," I said to Bill. "No furniture yet and no electricity but a spot to lay our heads."

"I'll get out the sleeping bags," he said. "You look for the candles. I think we have some in the brown suitcase."

Into our living room, that first evening, drifted the fragrance of white ginger. From the window we admired the cloud-capped *Volcán de Fuego de Colima,* its lower slopes sheathed in pine forests, its peak bare with forbidding rock and lava.

A tropical breeze ruffled the stand of bananas in the patio.

It was September. Heat wrapped around us snugly, like a blanket.

At dusk huge black and white moths soared lazily through unscreened rooms, while bands of mosquitoes hummed about. We remarked on the wealth of simple living things: spiders... ants.

"Did you see the daddy-long-legs?" Bill took me to an outside wall of the house where thousands of them clustered.

We blew out the candles early and settled down on the floor in our sleeping bags.

At three in the morning the storm hit. The rain came sideways, in sheets, through open windows and doors. With it came two lizards, a garter snake, and a little green frog which landed on my pillow. In two minutes the floor was an inch deep in water. Wind howled. We could hear the rattle of tiles falling from the roof, the thud of coconuts hitting the ground in the lot next door. Blinding lightning was followed by crescendos of thunder.

"The light plant must have blown up," Bill said. "Where is Sam?"

The next flash showed us the dog crouched in a corner, trembling, panting and slobbering. Zigzags of lightning gave us glimpses of trees bent almost double, banana fronds tearing at their stems.

The rain and wind stopped as suddenly as they had come; lightning and thunder moved away towards Manzanillo.

During the next few weeks we grew used to tropical rains. They came almost nightly. Bill made little comment. Once he did point out, "It rains only twenty inches a year in Berkeley."

I consulted the Triple A Guidebook. "That's how much it rains here," I said. "It just comes all at once." (I checked off on my mental Mexico list: perfect climate -well, not quite.)

Let There Be Light

"And then I stuck a knife in him. It went in here and it came out there."

Calisto, the night watchman for our Colima neighborhood, gently touched Bill on the ribs and side. "Not enough to kill. Too bad. *Qué lástima.*" He gave a horrible grimace and drew himself up to his full height, several inches shorter than Bill or me. "He was a thief, a real *ladrón* that one."

Calisto's scowl was replaced by a smile. His teeth glistened in the dim light. He leaned down to pat Sam. The dog, dozing under Bill's chair, snored softly, his hind legs jerking as he dreamed of the chase.

Calisto lit a cigarette, blew out the match and used it to flip a large spider off the table. "Well, anyway," he said, "I got him later. With a *pistola.* That's why I had to leave the village and drive a bus for *Flecha Amarilla.* Boring, but good pay."

The candles flickered as I laid a red six on a black seven. I could hear the frenzied buzzing of a beetle somewhere near the oil lamp on the bookcase. Bill and I had been sitting, these evenings, playing our endless solitaire, the only residents on a street without a name, in a house without lights, without screens, without a door between the kitchen and the street — a door due to arrive "any day" from Guadalajara. In the meantime we pushed the refrigerator around to fill the empty space.

Outside a half moon lighted the patio. Through the picture window, designed to frame a view of the volcano, I could make out a young pepper tree struggling to hold its own by the freshly laid sidewalk, and a burgeoning group of banana plants. I could smell burning sugar cane over the fragrance of the jasmine vine. The dominant smell, however, was *Doble Acción Raid* with which we fought mosquitoes nightly.

"You are playing that card game wrong," Calisto, who had been watching intently, informed us for the third time. "At *naipes* I'm the greatest. It goes like this."

The cards were quickly scattered in unfamiliar patterns. We were also in for another evening of gory tales of the State of Guerrero where Calisto had seen, in his younger days, more mayhem and murder than seemed possible.

Not only did we have no lights, no refrigeration, no electric fans as the temperature hovered at ninety. We also had as yet no curtains on the living room windows to keep passersby like Calisto from peering in.

"I knew you were lonely as soon as I looked in your window," Calisto said the first night, after knocking politely at the door. "I'm the *velador*, the night watchman for these blocks. It's a bad thing without lights, but some day the poles will come from Guadalajara, God willing. Meantime I'll keep you company in the evening... when I'm not working, that is."

He hefted his pistol on one hand and looked at it critically.

"I might be working at any minute. I thought I heard a suspicious noise in the banana trees in your patio. You should put your red ten here and the black six goes over there. You don't know a thing about cards, do you?"

Being suggestible types, Bill and I thought several times afterwards that we detected sinister rustlings in the banana trees. At those times Calisto was somewhere else.

We took daily walks with Sam, inspecting our new neighborhood. We lived between two worlds. On the one hand we were a block from the Calzada Galvan and the Governor's mansion, distinguished by its fierce Weimeraners and its somnolent security guards. This gave us class. On the other hand our street had yet to achieve real distinction; it was new and the paint had not had time to peel from the house facades. There were no trees over ten feet high as yet, nothing to compare with the lofty *parotas* and century-old palms of the Calzada. Beyond the new houses our street petered away into pure *monte*, undeveloped fields where goats roamed, pigs rooted, and small boys armed with slingshots wandered through the bushes waging war on us and on each other. Squatters squatted in half-built homes on future streets, their charcoal fires glowing dimly in the night. Iguanas, lizards of all hues, snakes and scorpions inhabited the empty lots. A bird cried plaintively in the sultry daytime, reciting over and over the capital of Iceland, "Reykjavik...Reykjavik."

"A bird of ill omen," Calisto told us. "We live in an evil world. I remember one time, when that bird sang in our village, my cousin was shot by a passing stranger... an argument in the *cantina*, nothing more. But for my cousin that bird called his death."

We slowly furnished our house, but no light poles arrived. Two weeks, three weeks. Any day now.

"I'm sorry. *Lo siento muchísimo.*" Manuel Gomez, our landlord, sighed. "Naturally I too would like the lights to go on. It's against the law to collect rent until light is provided, but the poles must first come from Guadalajara."

Colima, a hundred and fifty miles from Guadalajara, depends upon it like a baby on its mother. *No hay en Colima* (there is none in Colima) is the cry if one is seeking almost anything. Dog food, lamp shades, shoe laces, coffee pots. All are due any minute from Guadalajara.

So we passed the evenings with candles and oil lamps. Either can generate enough heat to melt by in a tropical climate. They did, however, light up the proud look on Calisto's face when he showed us, not for the first time, the ugly scar on his stomach, and recounted how he finally caught up with some *ladrón* or other.

We were, of course, aware that this Spartan existence in Mexico was not necessary. We could move on to Cuernavaca or Chapala, where visiting foreigners were expected, and easily rent a furnished place. But we liked being the only Americans within blocks, almost the only ones in the city. We had no recourse but to get acquainted with our neighbors and they, not prejudiced by an over-abundance of tourists, welcomed us as friends. In spite of material setbacks we had a growing fondness for Colima. Bill surprised me one day.

"I really like the place," he said. "Something about it gets to you. The people maybe."

I agreed. How can you dislike a city where you are immediately treated as a friend? Where Berto at the motel insists that, though you are no longer a guest, you swim in the motel pool each day, and sends an occasional steak from his restaurant to tide you over? Where Yolanda nearby shares space in her refrigerator, and Rosita round the corner provides ice cubes daily? A city where if you buy a table and have to ride home with it in the store truck (because you live on a new unnamed street and must show the way) the driver willingly waits while you visit the dry cleaner and shop at the market? A city where the small golf course seems to have been made for you alone, after years of waiting in line to tee off at any California course? A city snuggled against a volcano which belches, spits and comes alive, looming dark against the sun or shimmering romantically by moonlight?

We waited from early September until the end of October. Then the poles came from Guadalajara; a gang of men from the Light Commission strung the street wires and went away. It remained only to run lines to individual houses. Manuel Gomez dropped over and shook Bill's hand fondly, thinking perhaps that sometime soon he would have tenants who actually paid rent. He and Bill had a long-standing joke about our street and what its name would be.

"It will be called *Calle Gomez*, of course. I am the owner of these four beautiful houses, *verdad?*" Manuel would say.

"It will be *Calle Wakefield*," Bill always retorted. "We are the only people foolish enough to live on this street as yet, *verdad?*"

Calisto told us one evening, "The street has now been named. It is Mariano Azuela Street, but don't go looking for him around here. He was just a famous writer."

It came time to file our light contract. "Where is your *plano de luz?*" The clerk at the light company glanced up from his comic book. "Nothing doing without it."

Light plan. Manuel was as ignorant as we because it now appeared that the four beautiful houses really belonged to his brother Ernesto in Mexico City. Ernesto was hailed by phone, he in turn called the architect, the architect called the chief engineer who called Manuel. Manuel then counted the base plugs and ceiling outlets. We waited hopefully for action as soon as our contract was filed, though where it was filed who could say; the letter "W" for Wakefield does not appear in the Spanish alphabet. Now we needed light lines strung from street to house, which could only be done by the Colima light company. No waiting for Guadalajara here, but waiting for Colima was just as bad.

Calisto sympathized. Manuel sympathized.

"I'm Mexican, of course," Manuel said, "but I agree with the saying, 'In Mexico if you want something done, you must do it yourself.' Unfortunately I can't install the light lines."

"You mustn't just sit there waiting," Calisto told us. "You foreigners think if you ask for something it is right away going to happen. We know better. You phone the company every half hour. I'll do it for you tomorrow from the *cantina*." He did, but nothing happened.

"If it really gets bad," Calisto told us that night, as he jumbled the cards into a complex arrangement, "my sister Carmen's cousin Venancia is just like that with the assistant manager." He crossed his fingers and winked. "But I wouldn't like to disturb her except in an emergency. If you knew the light manager you would realize that she is always very busy. By the way," he added, "have you put up your *alambre* yet?"

"Our what?" Bill said.

"Don't you have an *alambre?*"

An *alambre* turned out to be a small but essential wire which, for mysterious reasons, the tenant of a new house must provide, inserting it in a pipe jutting up from the roof. Calisto kindly took care of it for us.

"I thought I had better tell you," he said. "Otherwise the light company men, who are well known to be *locos*, if they ever come will say, '*No hay alambre.* We can't put up the wires.' Then who knows when they will come again?"

Finally one morning two workmen suddenly showed up to string our street-to-house wires. All seemed set. We were getting ready to express gratitude. Then the short, permanently angry one opened the fuse box. His cry was frankly triumphant.

"*No hay fusibles!* We will not put up wires when there are no fuses."

We extracted a promise that the men would wait while we rushed downtown to buy *fusibles.*.Surely, certainly they would wait the ten minutes necessary. We returned in seven minutes flat to find them gone. They were never seen again.

That afternoon we went in search of Manuel Gomez. We found him drinking beer with an electrician who came over at once, strung the wires and connected the lights — illegally of course. Perhaps his ministrations were the reason why the electricity in that house was always erratic: on one day, off the next; now dim, now bright enough to blind.

"You see," I told Bill, "everything turns out all right. You just have to wait a little."

We blew out candles, turned on ceiling fans, started ice cubes congealing, and retired our solitaire cards forever. Calisto gave us up.

"I like you but you are terrible card players," he said, smiling to soften the blow. "You are never going to learn." He moved his activities to the *cantina*.

Nice Place to Visit, But I Wouldn't Want to Drive There

So far we'd had no trouble driving, but we remembered past vacations in Mexico when we'd taken car trips with our friend Ernesto. I recalled one such occasion vividly.

"Mexico is a wonderful country to visit," Bill said, as Ernesto barreled around a curve on Highway 15 between Tepíc and Mazatlán. "I wouldn't care to drive here though. Too many hazards."

Ernesto honked vigorously, squeezed by a second-class bus and edged into the traffic again.

"I've been driving here for thirty years," he said. "No problem. I've never had an accident." I closed my eyes. A herd of goats ahead had caused a traffic jam and we stopped just in time.

I hope I won't be riding with Ernesto when he has his first accident, I thought, though of course, being Mexican, he would know how to handle it better than a tourist. A visitor, I had heard, might land in jail for a long stretch while the authorities sorted things out in a leisurely fashion.

In the next town a policeman did flag us down - Ernesto had gone through a red light - and demanded menacingly to see car papers, Ernesto's papers, Bill's and my passports. Some money changed hands subtly, no papers were shown, and we sped on our way again.

"You have to hand out a *mordida* sometimes," Ernesto remarked. "Nobody's papers are ever entirely in order. It's not possible."

That was some years ago and Ernesto planned a visit to us in Berkeley, driving of course.

"You'll find things simpler in California when you come up to see us in April," I told him. "Rules laid out, no bribes, everything cut and dried. You'll have no trouble. Not so exciting, of course."

I laughed now, remembering what happened during Ernesto's visit. He reached our house in Berkeley without incident.

"Your superhighways," he said. "They are fast but very dull, *verdad*? I'll go for a drive around town tomorrow by myself and look the place over."

The next night he came home frowning. "Things in this country I don't understand." He tossed a slip of paper on the table. "A summons. What's that?"

Bill checked the paper.

"You parked at a meter that had expired," he explained. "You'll have to send in some money."

"Expired? I read that on the meter. I can read English perfectly well. But 'expired'? Means 'died,' yes? Means they don't use it any more. I'll just go down to your traffic court tomorrow and explain."

"Don't offer them money except for the fine," Bill said. "Remember you're in the United States where we do things the legal way."

Ernesto set forth again the next day and returned with another ticket: "Parked more than 18 inches from the curb."

"You said this is a free country? I must measure my distance every time I park? I have no ruler."

He went down to court again rather than send in the money as Bill suggested.

"It says here I am to appear so I will appear. In your country I do things legally. The *señorita* down there is not pretty but she has a nice smile."

The next day it was "parking in a red zone."

"Your police *señoritas*   move very fast." Ernesto scowled. "I parked on the red zone for a short time only. There was no other space."

As the days went on our guest became more irascible.

"Too many rules," he complained. "This is not a free country as you claim. I was going a little fast today but I wanted to get back here for supper." He pulled a crumpled ticket from his pocket. "Twenty dollars!"

Something about Ernesto caught the attention of every traffic cop and meter maid in the San Francisco Bay area. He became a fixture at traffic court.

"Why should I stop at a stop sign when no one is coming? Is that sensible?"

"Why should I not turn left on the red? I thought no one saw me."

It happened that our living room window looked out on a speed trap where automobiles which had been clocked at the top of the hill by a radar car were stopped at the bottom to receive their speeding tickets. Ernesto took to sitting morosely at the window in the evenings, counting the victims.

"I had thought of moving up here," he said. "Yours is a great country in many ways. But now I believe I will not."

A few days later he made his decision. He had gone through the same stop light which had brought him a ticket before, and had been stopped by the same policeman.

"I am leaving Saturday," he told us that night. "I have made my choice. I am now returning to a place of personal freedom."

"What happened this time!" Bill asked.

"That policeman remembered me from before. He said I should go to driving school. Me! After thirty years of driving in Mexico!"

Ernesto went home. The next time we visited him in Mexico he drove us around as usual. I shut my eyes at dangerous moments. After all, I thought, Ernesto has always made it. Why should he miss this time?

Sometimes he recalled his weeks in Berkeley.

"A beautiful country, interesting people, everything fast and efficient...but no...I am happy I did not move there. Here we have true freedom." He swerved around a burro which had wandered into the road, and stepped hard on the gas.

A Shopping Trip

We waited to buy furniture until our funds arrived from Berkeley, a matter of six weeks. Then we set out happily to furnish our home, which up to then had contained a couple of beds and some camping equipment.

We could not duplicate the conveniences of California. I had kissed goodbye to my freezer, dishwasher, electric stove, washing machine. I hoped to make up for this by buying things beautiful to look at. In Colima this is not easy, except for *"equipales"*, leather tables and chairs made by a local artisan, which are handsome and inexpensive. For folk art we would go to Guadalajara.

We decided to take our VW on the buying trip but to hire a driver. We were unfamiliar with the big city mysteries of Guadalajara shopping, and in Mexico hiring a licensed chauffeur is a poor man's treat; the going rate then was six dollars a day plus lunch.

"I can find you a chauffeur," Manuel Gomez said. "Just let me get the word around."

Very soon Aurelio turned up, striding across the empty lots north of our house, whistling and kicking at loose stones. He was a stocky young fellow wearing sandals, baggy brown pants, and a faded T-shirt with "Oakland Raiders" stenciled across the front. He removed his baseball cap and shook hands with Bill. Then he stood on our doorstep smiling proudly while Bill studied his chauffeur's license. It was Aurelio's license all right, although in the picture the mustaches looked fiercer and his hair, which must have been cut for the occasion, was a bristly black mat. The license read "Chauffeur, first category."

"I have been to many places," Aurelio explained as he pocketed the license. *"Tengo mucha experiencia.* To Tecomán... Coquimatlán... Atenquique... Armería."

"Guadalajara?"

"Of course. *Claro.*" He hesitated a moment. "Guadalajara too."

"See our combi there." Bill pointed to the VW parked in the driveway. He unconsciously adopted a childish tone and raised his voice. "The car. You can drive it? The car? Yes? You can surely drive it?"

Aurelio grinned.

"Sí, Señor." He made gestures of seizing a wheel and turning a few corners. "Very simple. I am a chauffeur. *Mucha experiencia."*

"And you know all the streets of Guadalajara... where the shops are and the big market? We want to go to Tlaquepaque too, the little town near the big city where they sell many things and mariachis play all day long. Tla-que-pa-que."

Bill's voice had risen some more, and I wondered if he thought the driver was deaf. Aurelio frowned, scratched his ear, smiled forgivingly.

"Don't you understand, *Señor,* that I am a licensed chauffeur? That is to say that I have been everywhere and if I have not, I find the way."

"Very well. We'll start early tomorrow. It's about four hours drive from here," Bill said.

"Three hours, *Señor.* Tomorrow very early." Aurelio strode off across country towards his home.

We were on our way at sun-up, leaving Colima on two-lane Highway 54. We passed lemon and orange groves, coconut plantations, small villages shaded by ancient palms, and the ugly sugarmill town of Queseria. Gradually with the flanks of the volcano on our left, we gained altitude. The sun became hotter. Out the window I saw jagged cliffs rising abruptly to a cloudless sky. We left sugarcane fields and banana groves to enter a terrain of rocks and pine trees. Now we wound up and up through big *barrancas,* deep dark ravines shrouded in huge trees and thick with underbrush. The highway dipped and climbed perilously.

"Go slower, Aurelio," said Bill, who was sitting in front. "We're not in a hurry."

"*Sí, Señor.*" Aurelio was whistling snatches of *El Relicario,* a *pasodoble* played at bull fights. He drove a little faster in order to pass a truck. He crossed himself and I noticed a crude shrine at the edge of the highway. Several names were carved on the rock below it and someone had left a bunch of fresh carnations.

"I know one of those," Aurelio said, crossing himself again. "*Tomás,* a *compadre* from my *barrio.* They passed a load of bananas and something in their car did not function. They went over the edge. *Los pobrecitos.*"

He crossed himself a third time, then went back to whistling.

"Aurelio!" Bill's voice rose.

"*Sí, Señor.*"

"Don't pass on curves, Aurelio. You know better than that. Slow down. What are you leaning out the window for?"

"*Sí, Señor.* That is my cousin who is just catching up with us, the one in the truck with the pigs in it...*Hola,* Nacho!"

Nacho hooted his horn and we sped around a sharp turn side by side. There was a screech of brakes. Sam, who had been sleeping on the baggage ledge behind me, slid forward onto my neck. We both yelped. A bus approaching the turn from the other direction barely missed us. Aurelio crossed himself with one hand, waved to the bus with the other.

We continued swooping around curves, wedging our way past buses, cars and trucks, passing roadside shrines. Aurelio kept busy crossing himself. Bill sat silent, grim, except for yelling from time to time, "SLOWER, AURELIO... SLOWER!... S L O W E R!"

Sam and I, huddled together, swayed from side to side of the combi as we barreled along.

"I think we will get there in less than three hours," Aurelio said.

"If we make it at all," Bill growled. "SLOWER!"

Finally our car got hung up behind a grunting second-class bus which emitted lethal fumes. We were very close.

A small boy standing on the back seat of the bus made a face at us and thumbed his nose.

"Aurelio," Bill cried, "keep your distance. Don't drive so close!"

I noticed that the bus had its name roughly scrawled in purple paint on the rear bumper: *"Sí Dios Quiere"*... "If God Wills."

Just then the bus jolted unexpectedly to a stop. We jolted to a stop too, just in time. Aurelio crossed himself twice and spat out the window. The boy in the bus stopped thumbing his nose and stuck out his tongue at us. An old man, an old woman, and a goat got off the bus. They disappeared into the bushes by the highway. I couldn't see any sign of road or habitation where they could be going.

Aurelio backed the car a little, to get around the bus.

Bill turned and faced me over the back of the front seat. "How in Hell do you say 'Stop tailgating' in Spanish?" "Don't know," I said. "Try a few curse words."

Bill's lessons at the language school in Oakland had not prepared him to express his feelings but he tried.

"Coño!" he shouted. Then he thought a minute. *"Chinga a tu madre!* DON'T FOLLOW SO CLOSE!"

"Sí, Señor. You speak very good Spanish. Since you are a foreigner you do not understand the words. I follow close so that I can pass that *cabrón."* He passed, swerving for an oncoming motorcycle.

It wasn't until we reached a detour outside Ciudad Guzmán that we discovered our chauffeur was illiterate.

"Look out, Aurelio," I called. "Didn't you see the sign?" We had sped past a big sign *DESVIACION,* and were plowing our way through a rough road where work was in progress.

"Sí, Señora, claro. I saw that sign."

"What did it say?"

"I don't know, *Señora."*

"You don't know? It said *'desviación'*...detour. Go back before we get stuck here."

Aurelio backed and we returned to the detour cutoff. "Now read that sign, Aurelio," Bill said severely. Aurelio scratched his head.

"I can't tell you what it says, *Señor."*

"You are a chauffeur first category, but you have never been to school? You can't read?"

"Of course I can read." He revved up the motor and plunged off into the detour. "I just don't know exactly what the words say, *Señor.* That is all."

We read signs to him until we were on the outskirts of Guadalajara and here we had another surprise.

"Turn right," Bill said as we approached the cutoff to go downtown.

Aurelio frowned and veered toward the left.

"Right! Right!" Nothing happened until Bill made a sweeping motion with his hand.

"Ah, sí, that way." Aurelio got back in the righthand lane by some miracle, and made the turn.

"Which is your left hand, Aurelio?" Bill asked when we stopped at the next stop light.

Aurelio frowned horribly. He pouted and shook his head. Then he raised his right hand from the wheel.

"I see," Bill said. "At least you know your way around this city, I hope. We want to go directly to the big market downtown."

Aurelio sped through streets and around turns, sometimes backing up when we went the wrong way on a one-way street. As we drove along in the stream of traffic a big statue of Minerva caught my attention. It was in the middle of a round place where streets came in and circled, an arrangement known in Spanish as a *glorieta.* We passed the Minerva *glorieta* five times. Then we came to a triumphant halt at the downtown market.

We forgot our car problems as we selected mirrors, lamps, rugs, pottery, all the things which, on our vacations in Mexico, we had been unable to carry back on the plane. We ate a picnic in the car while Aurelio went off to a food stand in the market.

After lunch we headed for Tlaquepaque, reaching it without incident. Aurelio shouted to passersby for instructions at the end of each block. Our shopping done, the car crammed with purchases, we started home, encountering with surprising ease our Highway 54.

The couple of beers which Aurelio had obviously had for lunch steadied him on the homeward trip. It was a smooth rollercoaster ride down hill most of the way. We were tired and even dozed a little except when awakened by a sharp turn as we swooped through the *barrancas,* and once by a sudden halt as a flock of goats crossed the highway.

At home Bill handed over money, and Aurelio returned the car key.

"Thank you for driving us, Aurelio," Bill said. "We won't need you again. We know the way now."

"Thank you, *Señor.*" Aurelio counted the money carefully. He jammed his baseball cap down on his head. "I now have more *experiencia* than before. Even more *experiencia.* I have now been for the first time in Guadalajara."

In the Market

Our guiding angel was Mina, the girl at the motel who had let us in with our dog. She moved to a job as receptionist at the Banco de Londres downtown. This job required her to look pretty and charming, no strain, and to help clients with any banking questions they might have. Mine were not routine banking questions.

"Where can I buy a lampshade without a lamp under it? ...How do I ask for a sprinkler attachment for the hose?... Where is the best place to get a watch repaired?...Is there anywhere in Colima to buy kibbled dog food?"

Mina greeted each question with a smile, put a finger to her nose while she thought a moment, and always came up with a good answer. This went on daily for about a month. Her only reference to bank matters was her suggestion each time I came in: "Aren't you thinking of moving your money from your country to a savings account here? Won't you do that just for me?"

I put her off, and just about the time I had finished my questions — the last one was "Where can I buy a nice box of chocolates?" (for Mina) — she married an architect and quit the bank for Mexico City. I ate the chocolates myself.

When our house was furnished, Bill turned his attention to the patio. He planted plants new to us: papayas which would bear fruit in a few months, a mango and a guava tree. An itinerant plant man dropped in to help Bill in his choices and we learned local names for many plants: a handsome blueflowered vine with very long sharp thorns called "the widow," flowers called "puppy dog" and "baby," and one vine named "the bedbug" whose small, dark leaves would spread and turn up everywhere.

I found that Mexican shopping is a time-consuming task. At least two hours every morning I devoted to errands. The supermarket for pasteurized milk, coffee, canned goods. The open market for a riot of tropical fruits and vegetables. The fish market for prawns or crayfish or red snapper brought in from the Pacific in the dawn hours. The bakery for rolls or sweet breads. Trips to the bank, the dry cleaner, the gas station. It was necessary to drive a mile downtown to post a letter since there are no corner mailboxes in Colima. What happened to that retirement leisure under a palm tree? Mexicans think it odd that Americans are so keen about native markets. Indeed there is a fascination about the open market even after one has lived some time in Mexico. Every Mexican town has special market days. The best time in Colima is very early on Wednesday or Sunday morning. The selection is probably at its best at five-thirty, but I have never arrived before seven.

I join one of the approaching groups of shoppers. With me is a visiting friend from the United States — her first visit, she views everything with interest. A covey of police cars is parked outside the big market, their drivers reading newspapers and watching for action. So far as I know there never is any action requiring police. They must go there just to gossip, have a cup of coffee, catch up on the news. Produce trucks squeal to a halt, boys pedal by on bicycles with huge flat baskets of rolls perched on their heads. Sidewalk vendors of flowers, cucumbers, mangos, hawk their wares. I pass stands where clothespins, coat hangers, sieves and paring knives are heaped. A strong smell of prawns, red snapper and Pacific ocean meets me from the line of fish booths.

In the market each little cubbyhole is a separate stall rented from the city, and each has its specialty. There is the egg girl, the chicken lady, the old witch who sells magic medicinal herbs, the machete man with his armory of knives. On the stands sit baskets of strawberries, heaps of papayas and pineapples. Oranges, tangerines, mangos, apples and guavas, have been polished and tastefully arranged in pyramids. Green beans, sweet onions with the stems on, peppers of all kinds, tomatoes, sweet potatoes. Overhead hang bunches of bananas, and underfoot lies the trash which collects each day — wilted lettuce leaves, squashed grapes. Children scamper around between the stalls, and the occasional dog forages.

In the rear of the market are the meat stalls with hunks of meat, unidentifiable by our standards of cut, hanging from hooks, while tables in front hold pigs feet and tripe. A couple of live iguanas, trussed and hung up for sale, take their last looks at a cruel world.

There is a beautiful section of dry groceries in baskets: pink beans, brown beans, yellow beans, black beans, rice and garbanzos. Almost in the middle of the market is the eating section, where little tables hold charcoal braziers with steaming corn on the cob, hot tacos, pots of stew.

There are goodies in the market which one has to be around for a while to appreciate, such as the round pieces of *"piloncillo,"* a hard brown sugar. In season there is sugarcane to chew, or nopal cactus leaves to boil. Grapefruit here are the size of basketballs. I skip the piles of unfamiliar little yellow, red, or purple fruits which are appreciated by the locals but not by me. They all taste bland and interchangeable.

On other unfamiliar foods I get hooked. Take my favorite fruit, a fruit I had never heard of before I came to Colima. I remember that day when, accompanied by my visiting friend, we made our tour of the market while I searched especially for it, the first of the season.

"Can I help you? Help you?" Two small boys competed to carry my basket. Shaking my finger negatively I squeezed through the crush of shoppers, for I was a little late in arriving on a busy Sunday. I stepped over a stray cantaloupe, slipped on rotted cabbage leaves, called *"Buenos días"* to my ancient friend, the tortilla woman, ducked to avoid a passing crate of tomatoes, and came to a forced halt at one of the vegetable stands. My visiting friend followed close behind, reaching out to grab my arm where the crowd was thick. At the vegetable stand a young girl loaded potatoes, onions, dark green chiles and pale green *chayotes* into the shopping bag of a hugely fat woman in a pink *rebozo*, who blocked the whole aisle ahead. On top of the bag the girl tossed a handful of coriander and one of mint, adding a subtle herb smell to the heavy carnation scent from the flower stall." *Qué va a llevar?"* she called to me, but I pushed my way around the fat woman, my friend following in my wake. I didn't need anything here. I was looking for black *zapotes* , the best fruit in the world. In the background I heard the blind man with his guitar singing *Cielito Lindo* off-key, and a fellow near him beating madly on a marimba. Children offered me birds in cages, hot tortillas, flopping puppets on a stick. But I was only interested in the best fruit in the world.

The fruit stand was packed with big orange papayas, little green limes, guavas the color of saffron. Overhead hung clusters of huge *macho* bananas, half black and ready for baking. The smell of pineapple dominated the stall. In one corner I spotted a mound of fruit the size of oranges but green-black, smooth-skinned. They looked like deflated balloons and were squashy to the finger. I, however, saw through this disguise. I knew how delicious they were. The shriveled old man chose three for me, *bueno para hoy* - just right for today — and poked them to prove it.

"These are perfect," I said to my friend. "Just wait until you try them!"

At home I cut the *zapotes* in half, removed the circles of large seeds, and spooned the sticky pudding-like black mass into a bowl.

I added a little sugar, some orange juice, a dash of rum. Now! The perfect dessert. Ambrosia.

I offered a dish to my guest. She made a suspicious face, tried a small spoonful.

"You'll love this," I told her again. "It's the best fruit in the world."

She laid down her spoon.

"It looks and tastes like mud," she said.

Intercambio

While Colima is a city of 90,000 people, I know of only six foreigners among them. English is taught in all the schools and everyone agrees it is the most useful second language. Without a chance to practice, however, there are few fluent speakers.

So when Bill and I, after we had got settled in our new home, suggested an *"intercambio"* — an exchange of Spanish and English conversation in a social setting — we were taken up on it with enthusiasm by some of our new acquaintances.

Three couples arranged to come to our house every Wednesday evening: Nicasio and Ilse, a doctor and his wife; Sergio, secretary of the state police force and his wife Stella; Gonzalo and Mari Lu, a young couple doing graduate work at the University. We awaited their first visit with interest. I laid in some cookies from the supermarket and made coffee.

We said good evening in our language and the others replied politely in theirs. We then changed roles so that we said *"Buenas noches,"* and our guests answered, "Good evening, how are you?" But English conversation, after the entering wedges, broke down quickly every Wednesday. As our friends put it, "You Americans aren't afraid to try to speak Spanish. We Mexicans are different. We are easily ashamed and don't want to make mistakes." We took their point, although we suspected that the dictum "Fools rush in..." was applicable to us Americans.

We found lots of interest to talk about in some language, and so we learned quite a bit of Spanish and the fiction was successfully maintained that an exchange was going on.

Nicasio brought his rare and beautifully illustrated books on Mexican plants and discussed the folklore of medicine with Bill. Here they had common ground in medical Latin and got on admirably.

Gonzalo was studying business administration. He practiced it by developing a lemon ranch a few miles from town. Judging from the bushels of lemons he dropped in my lap (there are only limited uses for lemons, I found), his course must be going swimmingly. I expect he will get some esoteric degree in lemonology.

Sergio, a forthright and outgoing character, looked to me at once like a useful friend should I ever be in dire need. Who, when driving in Mexico, has not thought with a shiver of a possible accident and its probably horrifying aftermath — furious policemen, jail cells, maybe thumbscrews. How about having a magic name, like Sergio Llamas, Secretary of the Police Force, *my friend* Sergio Llamas to fling in the face of the law? I did not court trouble, but I felt less terrified when I narrowly missed a bicycle darting into the street without warning, or got wedged between two second-class buses staging a downtown race.

I was brought up very strictly, however, and I find it impossible to park knowingly in the wrong places or to go the opposite way on a one-way street. Nobody else in Colima minded doing these things, and all the traffic cops were armed with pliers and screwdrivers, not to tweak the noses of offenders but for the mundane purpose of removing license plates. One license plate per offense, and the whole car towed away for the third infraction. I would say that about a quarter of the cars in Colima had no license plates. In a relaxed, tropical city it's a terrible amount of trouble to go all the way down to the police station to pay the fine and retrieve the plates.

My only brush with the law generated no excitement. The Wednesday before I had been discussing with Sergio the different traffic laws in Mexico and California. I happened to ask him about turning right on a red light, after a stop, if the traffic permits it. We can do this in California, but I had never been certain about Colima. There are not too many traffic lights there, five or six maybe, and Sergio told me there was just one, the one where I always turned right to go down to the market, where it was permitted to circulate to the right on a red signal. The next morning I did so, only to hear a piercing police whistle behind me. It must have come from the traffic policeman standing on the corner. I had the distinct feeling that it was a call for me, but since there were other cars around perhaps infringing on some law, I decided to ignore it.

That is the trouble with being unique in a place like Colima. The next morning the same cop was on duty at a different corner. He flagged me down.

"You made a mistake yesterday," he told me severely. "You turned right on Pino Suarez when the light was red. Don't say you didn't. There is no other VW combi in town with you in it." He reached menacingly for his pliers.

"It was me in it," I conceded, "but *my friend,* Sergio Llamas, who-is-practically-the-head-of-your-police force, told me I could turn right there."

Frowning, the officer walked away.

"Don't do it again," he called back over his shoulder.

The next day there was a new sign at the corner of Pino Suarez, indicating a right turn allowed on a red light. My young policeman lolled against this sign. He pretended not to see me. I resisted the impulse to lean out and yell, "I told you so!"

Our *intercambio* evenings went on pleasantly once the initial timidity wore off. We, as brash Americans, learned a little more Spanish every week and the belief in an interchange was supported by each Wednesday's initial gambit, *"Buenas noches,"* from us, "Good evening," from them, and each Wednesday's parting shot, *"Hasta Miércoles"*..."See you next Wednesday."

Among us wives, meantime, the *intercambio* turned imperceptibly into an inter-cookery or culinary contest. It was agreed that each couple should take turns bringing some snack or other, while we provided coffee. My supermarket cookies were immediately put in their place by Mari Lu's coffee cake, and this was followed by Stella's tacos. Gradually the idea expanded. What started as a snack stayed to become a banquet. Salad was added, then jello (a favorite Mexican item). Sometimes *sopitos* or *tamales* from the House of Ten Flavors were offered, along with *atole,* a rather juvenile-tasting drink made from milk and cornmeal. Mari Lu specialized in macaroni salad while Stella became known for her custard *flan.*

Ilse, the doctor's wife, had something really special to offer. Not always the same thing, but always something different. Her passion turned out to be serving anything so long as it looked like something else. The first hint of this came early in the game, when she produced an excellent moist white cake.

"What do you think it is?" she asked me in Spanish, then, to make sure, in English. "Is...what?" "Is sponge cake," I told her. "Very good. In fact *muy sabroso*. In fact *riquísimo.*"

She burst into a delighted giggle.

"Not so. Not at all. This cake is made with spaghetti!"

I expressed surprise and admiration. I asked for the recipe but of course it was a secret. I have since tried to duplicate with various additions of flour, eggs, sugar, but my spaghetti remained essentially itself.

I asked Ilse if she could make spaghetti out of cake but, after a burst of laughter, she turned the conversation to other things.

As the weeks went by Ilse's surprises were various: chocolate pudding made without chocolate; cookies simulating potato chips; tamales which turned mysteriously into apple dumplings.

It got so I couldn't trust Ilse about anything. Every time a few of her ten children turned up to escort their parents home I would look very carefully to be sure they were children. Not chipmunks or rabbits in disguise?

Her greatest triumph was saved for my birthday, when she brought along a large platter of poached eggs. Poached eggs??? The plate did seem to contain eggs when she brought it in the front door. Ilse set down the food and burst into a million snickers.

"Try it!"

It turned out to be a tray covered with custard and on that, neatly arranged, a series of upside-down peach halves.

When Christmas came, gifts were exchanged over a supper including everybody's specialty: my apple pan-dowdy, Mari Lu's tacos, Stella's multicolored custard, and Ilse's meatless meat loaf. What our husbands thought, I don't know. They ate it.

Small presents were passed around: a toy kitten, a potted fern, a wooden kangaroo for holding toothpicks. Ilse's present to me was a useful-looking ballpoint pen. Could this be? Her smile showed me that all was not as simple as it seemed. "Chanel No. 5" was printed on the barrel and a delicate whiff of perfume soon filled the room.

Eventually it came time for summer vacation. Sergio and Stella were taking their four children on a jaunt to Disneylandia; Nicasio and Ilse were going out for a while to their ranch; Gonzalo and Mari Lu were planning to grow some outsized lemons. We would all be meeting again in a month, but Ilse brought me a farewell present anyway. It was a clay figure shaped like a llama. With it came a packet of seeds.

"Look," Ilse said, "you wet the llama with water like this. Then rub in the seeds. Keep the hollow inside full of water and in a few days the seeds will sprout. Wait and see."

Sure enough, within a week the llama was covered with green foliage (looked like bean sprouts sort of; in Spanish it's called *chia*) a couple of inches long.

"What's that llama doing with grass growing on it?" Bill asked.

I had been fully indoctrinated by now.

"That's not grass, silly," I told him. "That's llama hair."

Nineteen Kids and No Pencil

Coat hangers, extension cords, film, golf balls, clothes pins, Dijon mustard, kitchen matches...My list of things to buy was carefully thought out and long. With the VW to tote my purchases I didn't want to forget anything. We had been living in Colima for six months and were heading back to California to renew our tourist visas. Then we would enter again and apply to take up residence as *inmigrante rentistas*, a permit allowing us to live in Mexico without frequent trips to the border.

Going up the 2300 miles to Berkeley we planned to travel light: just ourselves, Sam the dog, and seven guitars. Mexican guitars are popular in the San Francisco Bay area, and we expected to make enough on these, even after paying duty, to help cover the cost of our journey.

A couple of hours before we left I dropped over to tell my friend Rosita that we would be gone for a month and to remind her to water our plants.

"How lucky you are going to the United States. Oh, I wish...*No importa*. Never mind."

"Can we bring you something from California?"

I thought about my list and how full the car would be but after all she was taking care of the plants. I could certainly bring some little thing.

"Well, yes, some drip-dry sheets, king size, six sets with flowers. Big towels to match."

As I was leaving she called after me. "Do you mind if I phone my sister Mariki?"

Mariki soon turned up at our house in a new white Renault car. We promised to oblige her as far as we were able, with lace-trimmed guest towels, plastic flowers, rolls of ribbon to make little fish figures, and magnetic strips to fasten these as decoration on her refrigerator. She wrote down on my scratch pad the colors, sizes and prices.

Mariki was followed in five minutes by Yolanda and our list in my notebook grew to include cranberry sauce, blueberry pie mix and a big sack of Milky Ways for her five kids.

Mari Lu and Stella had already put in their bids for Corningware. Dr. Nicasio needed a special battery for his ophthalmascope. Sergio felt it would be easy for us to find a windbreaker exactly like the one he had seen on sale in San Diego three years ago.

As we were leaving the house the telephone rang. "Don't answer it," Bill said and locked the door.

***

Though parts of Mexico are heavily populated, there are also miles of primitive countryside where there is no one, or perhaps just a cabin or two back in the bushes, a corn field, a patch of maguey, a burro.

We were on such a deserted stretch, between Tepíc in the mountains and Mazatlán on the coast. I had been driving. It came time to change places and I stopped the car and turned off the ignition. When Bill got into the driver's seat and turned the key nothing happened. We are both in a mechanical category where all we know is that our VW engine is in the rear of the car. However, we dutifully got out, looked the engine over, got in again and tried the starter. No action. We did this several times, then sat in the car wondering what else to do. Several cars whizzed by. None stopped.

It was afternoon and darkness would come in an hour or two. We remembered scary stories of bandits on this very highway who raid foreign cars and strip them of everything. In our case they wouldn't get much unless they wanted to start a mariachi band with seven guitars.

The view, while lonely, was a splendid one. A vast stretch of low rolling hills clad lightly in cactus, pepper trees, tamarinds and scrub mesquite, with an occasional cornfield making a patch of green and cattle making spots of black. In the distance lofty gray-blue mountains.

There were no houses in sight. There was no one walking on

the road. No more cars passed..

Suddenly a squeaky voice came from nowhere.

"My name is Rodolfo. What are you called?"

I couldn't see anyone. Do bandits usually introduce themselves? I stuck my head out the window and there was Rodolfo, squatting beside the car. He was wearing an oversized pair of chopped-off pants. He looked about nine years old.

"Where's your father, Rodolfo," I said. "Where's the town you live in? Our car doesn't want to start and we need a mechanic."

Rodolfo repeated his first statement. In order to speed things up I said, "My name is Celia."

Bill, on the driver's side of the car, was engaged in conversation, too. I heard the words "Julio...Jesús...Luis".

In a few minutes there were nineteen — I counted them — small boys, none more than ten years old, and some barely able to

walk. They swarmed over us, staring in windows, climbing onto the roof, crawling under the chassis. There were no adults with them. I got out of the car and took Rodolfo by the shoulder.

"Our car is discomposed," I told him urgently. "It doesn't want to start. We must find a mechanic quickly. Where do you live?"

"I can write my name, which is Rodolfo," he told me at once, "but I have no pencil. Have you a pencil?"

The crowd of kids closed in around me. Rodolfo gestured at them.

"My friends," he said.

I felt in my pocket.

"I did have a pencil," I told Rodolfo, "but I lost it in Tepíc." I could hear echoings in the crowd of children.

"She lost it in Tepíc...Where?...In Tepíc."

Rodolfo picked up a small stick from the side of the road. In a patch of sand he painstakingly scrawled an R.

"Now the mechanic...the town," I said. "There must be a town?"

Rodolfo added an O to the R in the sand. "We can all write our names," he told me, "except the small ones." He gestured disdainfully at Juanito in the bushes. "But we have no pencils. And we have no paper. Are you sure you have no pencil?"

"I have no pencil," I said firmly. "Not now. If we could possibly find a mechanic my husband might have a pencil."

"Under the palm tree," Rodolfo said. He finished writing his name in the sand. A dozen shrill voices said, "Under the palm tree."

"Where is the palm tree? Do you really think there is a mechanic under it?"

"Yes, we will take you there. But afterwards the pencil."

A detachment of seven little boys escorted me, four in front and three behind. Bill and Sam stayed in the car to entertain the other twelve boys. Sam reacts with fury to any strange hand at the car window. Faced with a couple of dozen miniature hands he lay down and pretended to sleep.

Looking back I could see children peering in windows, toying with windshield wipers, kicking tires, jumping up and down on bumpers. Looking ahead I noticed a lone coconut palm with a man sitting under it. Beside him lay what looked like a heap of car parts.

"There," said Rodolfo, pointing proudly, "a mechanic."

"Are you a mechanic?" I asked, when we reached the tree.

"No, I am not a mechanic. I just like engines. And parts of engines."

"Will you look at our engine? It doesn't want to work, and we are trying to get to Mazatlán before dark. Will you come and look at it please?"

"It's too far away."

"No it isn't, it's right over there."

The man yawned and got to his feet.

"Well, if it's that close."

Twenty minutes later he had finished tinkering.

"Try the car," he said. It started! It worked! "It ought to get you into Mazatlán; that's only 70 kilometers and you can get real repairs there. If you stop, keep the engine running."

We paid him generously and prepared to get under way.

"My pencil!" cried Rodolfo. "Our pencils!" all the children yelled. Bill and I looked carefully through our pockets and around the car. No pencils.

"But here's some change to buy pencils." Bill handed over coins. The crowd of children melted quickly away. The mechanic had already returned to his palm tree. We left.

Very soon we realized that something was wrong. As a dog, Sam is smarter than we are about some things. He ran to and fro on the back seat whining and barking and looking upward, then at us, accusingly.

Sam can't stand to see us robbed of anything, even the garbage, and this was his warning behavior. Bill stopped the car, keeping the engine running, and we checked for what might be missing. The guitars were all there, the camera on its shelf, Bill's wallet was in his jacket. But we seemed to hear someone shouting.

Bill got out and immediately discovered a clue hanging over the edge of the car roof — a small bare foot. Following it up he came on Rodolfo crouched in the baggage well on top of the camper, his eyes closed tight, his mouth wide open for a howl which presently came.

"Come down, Rodolfo. I'll help you."

Another howl as the boy's hands tightened on the brackets at the edge of the well. No getting him down. We turned and headed slowly back the few miles to the palm tree, keeping in mind that Rodolfo was riding the roof.

The mechanic was fitting two pieces of metal together. He looked up and scowled, "What happened?" Then he saw our cargo.

"Rodolfo!"

"Papa!" Rodolfo climbed down and they were fondly reunited.

"My son, I didn't even know you were gone. Rodolfo, my life, you have come back to me!" cried Papa.

Rodolfo gave a sob. They clung to each other. Papa looked up at the camper.

"So high! So dangerous. What a journey!" Rodolfo gave a louder sob.

While searching the glove compartment for a piece of kleenex to dry my tears at this affecting reunion I came on a stub of pencil. I picked it up and stuck out my arm to Rodolfo.

"Here, Rodolfo. Here's your pencil. I didn't lose it in Tepíc after all."

He leaped forward, grabbed the pencil, and gave me a wide grin. Before the car could start moving, however, this changed to a frown. Then his mouth opened for another yell. "Paper! I have no paper!"

I pulled out an old scratch pad from the glove compartment and tossed it to him. "Here's your paper. Adiós, Rodolfo."

We had driven some miles before I realized that I had thrown Rodolfo the pad containing the list of purchases for our Colima friends: Nicasio's battery number, the size and colors of Mariki's fish ribbons, the name of Yolanda's blueberry pie mix. The pad also had important phone numbers to call, a notation of Bill's eyeglass prescription, the address of a friend in Nogales.

"Well, anyway," I told Bill, "I won't forget the sack of Milky Ways for Yolanda's covey of kids. For the rest, it's sort of a relief."

Nicasio's House

After some months in Colima we decided, spurred on by our *intercambio* friends, that we were paying too much for too little where we lived. The house, though new, was small and cramped. The builder had included a front yard instead of designing the house around a central patio. A picket fence surrounded this yard, reminding me of my childhood in New England. Nothing else reminded me of it. Not the burgeoning banana trees which grew at nightmare speed tangling up the telephone lines and dropping brown muddy sap on anyone underneath; not the struggling pepper tree by the sidewalk which gained a foot only to be pruned a foot by passing goats. Not the endless procession of shoeshine boys, girls selling tortillas, old women offering crocheted baby clothes, and occasional wanderers in ragged pants and worn *huaraches* who would like to promote "just enough pesos to make it to Guadalajara."

We sat in our back patio but it was small, especially as the roses, bougainvillea and papaya trees grew like lightning, filling most of the space. In the patio we heard all the noises of a closed-in Mexican neighborhood. Next door America, the aviator's wife, spanked little

America who howled. Beyond that Arnolfo, the engineer, worked on his antique car, mostly revving up the engine and blowing the horn. On the other side the mosquito lady (so called because of her fancy screens) practiced runs and trills to improve her soprano voice. Children in neighboring patios played ball games in the twilight and far into the night. Over all hung the persistent smell of chiles and hot fat.

"You would prefer Villa de Alvarez," Gonzalo told us at one of our Wednesday evening talk sessions. "It is very tranquil there."

"It happens that I am just now building a house in La Villa," Nicasio remarked. "It is almost ready."

"Yes," Sergio said. "We have all seen it. Such a beautiful house. One of the best in Villa de Alvarez."

"We have all seen it many times." Mari Lu sounded worried. "But are you sure our friends would be happy on that street? It is very close to the *barrio*."

"But only one block from the plaza," Nicasio pointed out. "And the *barrio* is very quiet. Nobody there will make trouble."

After more discussion it was unanimously decided that Bill and I would be happy in Villa de Alvarez even though it would of course not have the sophistication of Colima. We already knew it as a separate little town attached to Colima like a small excrescence, as the Colimans viewed it, or like a superior jewel as the people of La Villa believed. Its streets were small and dusty; its view of the volcano over neighboring cornfields superb; its main plaza very large, tree-shaded and rose-filled, with an elaborate church in the middle — five separate domes on top, all colored gold. We knew the little town as the place where party-givers in Colima went to buy excellent *tamales, atole,* and *tuba,* a local drink made from palm sap.

"But we can't move right out of here," Bill objected. "We have no lease as such, but we do have to give ninety days notice. Nobody would hold a house for rent that long." Mari Lu shrugged, indicating, "So what?"

"The thing is," I explained, "we had to put down three extra months rent as a deposit. We lose it if we move out without proper notice."

"Oh, you paid money. That's different."

"No importa." Nicasio smiled amiably, revealing a gold tooth among the gleaming white ones. "The house is not finished, although nearly. So we can wait a little while. Drive out there and look at it. You can drop in at my *consultorio* on the way. I have an interesting heart case coming in tomorrow."

Nicasio and Ilse lived in Colima where Nicasio had an office in his home. His other office in Villa de Alvarez was open afternoons. He knew everyone in the little town.

"You will like it in Villa de Alvarez," he said. "Very tranquil. A fine small Mexican town."

Ilse took us out to the house the next day. We made an immediate decision that this was the place for us. It was not like the cottage we were living in where everything was small and hot. This house had a big interior patio with a colonnade, or *portal,* around it, a large back yard, airy rooms with lots of windows, an old-fashioned kitchen big enough to eat in as well as cook in. It was half the price of our Colima cottage.

Behind the back yard, through a break in the wall, was the corral. It held only one horse now, a tired-looking grey mare in a thatched stall.

"We have three fine horses at the ranch," Ilse told us. "You will see them when the fiesta comes. Naturally we will put a gate where the hole in your wall is."

Sam, off the leash, ran wildly through the corral flushing a chicken and two cats. Bill and I strolled around in this country atmosphere. The corral was big and unkempt and beautiful. Seven palms towered over it. Ilse said they were at least a hundred years old. A *primavera* tree covered solidly with yellow flowers grew alongside a jacaranda, smothered at this season in purple blooms. An enormous mango tree drooped under its weight of ripening fruit. The combined smell of horse manure, mint from a patch growing by the wall, and some unidentified flowering vine, was not unpleasant. In one corner of the corral moss-covered bricks surrounded a well. Birds chirped in the thickets. I tried to identify them for I had just finished reading a pamphlet on Colima birds. A russet-crowned motmot, perhaps? A cinnamon flower-piercer?

They looked more like sparrows and swallows, except for two iridescent green hummingbirds poised over a young *guanábana* tree.

Of course, the house was not finished. It lacked window frames, doors, a floor. It had walls and a roof, which looked weatherbeaten for a new house, I thought, but buildings age quickly in the tropics. What could be more convenient than a house that was not yet ready. We could give proper notice at the old place, and also watch our new home in its final stages.

We made another trip to Villa de Alvarez with Nicasio and Ilse and explained our timing carefully. Ninety days notice.

"I'll ask the *maestro* here when this house will be done," Nicasio said.

The *maestro* looked up from the tiles he was laying in the kitchen. There was a consultation in low tones.

"Perfectly all right," Nicasio assured us. "The *maestro* says it will be ready long before ninety days. We will hold it for you, or you can move in and we won't charge rent until your time at the other place is finished."

"You're sure it will be ready?"

"*Seguro!* " The *maestro* slapped a spadeful of cement between some tiles. "*Claro. Qué le vaya bien, Señor.*"

"All right," Bill said."We'll count on it then. We'll give notice today."

"*Seguro!*" cried Nicasio. "*Andale, pues. Qué le vaya bien.*"

Houses were in short supply in Colima. As soon as we gave notice a new tenant for our old house was found, to move in the day we would leave. We took to going out on Sundays to see how our home was coming. The *maestro* did not work on Sundays, but during the week he was evidently busy. Each Sunday another few feet of tiling had been laid. Since the tile was of an intricate shape and had to be fitted into corners and around doorways, it was a tough task. After five weeks, as the floor progressed with caterpillar speed, we decided to drop in on a week day and confer with the *maestro.*

"When will it be done?" The *maestro* looked surprised, thoughtful, as though such a question had never been asked before. He stroked his mustache. He frowned. "When will it be done? *Quién sabe?* There is much to do. You can see that for yourselves." He wiped a sleeve across his sweaty face. "I have Alfredo here as *mozo* and we are working hard. *Quién sabe?*"

We waited another week, noticed a little more work had been done. Then Bill telephoned Nicasio.

"We just wanted to ask about the house. It will be ready on time? There doesn't seem to be much progress."

"Of course it will be ready. I guarantee it." Nicasio sounded hurt. "Would I tell you the house would be ready if it wouldn't be? Would the *maestro* say so?"

"The *maestro* says, '*Quién sabe?*'"

"If it will not be ready I will certainly hire more workmen."

Time marched on the way it always does and we were only two weeks from moving day. Lacking a ready house on that day we would find ourselves in the street with a load of furniture and no place to go. I called Ilse.

"Of course it will be ready. Don't worry. We guarantee it." Her voice was gay and forgiving. "We are all going to pitch in and work. Nicasio has hired another helper. *Seguro!*"

We checked the house again. The *maestro* had two new helpers. This seemed to lead to more talk and less work all around.

Bill made a list of things still to be finished: doors, window frames and glass, bathroom fixtures, garage. The list looked suspiciously like the list of unfinished work of almost three months before. I called Nicasio and treated him to a fit of *gringo* hysteria.

"An impossible situation! You promised me! You have failed us!" And so on.

Nicasio made soothing noises, murmured more promises, and we hung up.

On going to the house that Sunday, with three days left until moving day, we found Nicasio, Ilse, and five of their children hard at work putting white paint on walls, ceilings and, inadvertently, floors.

"*Casi listo!* Almost ready!" Nicasio greeted us with a warm smile. "The doors are ordered, the windows are coming. Here's the plumber now — Sr. Zepeda. We're just waiting for the fixtures to arrive from Guadalajara."

We did move on moving day. We had to. After we had been in the house for a few hours the plumbing fixtures arrived from Guadalajara. Sr. Zepeda, who was waiting over a can of beer, quickly installed them.

Bill hurried at once to the bathroom and slammed the door. "That was just in time," he said, when he came out. "Now if they'll just get around to putting on a front door." Nicasio dropped in.

"The lights are on, I see," he said, trying one. "I gave a small *mordida*. I wouldn't want you to be without light. There's not much left to do now...the garage, the patio wall, the kitchen counter..."

"How about a front door?" I complained. "We can't sleep here with the house wide open, can we?"

Nicasio looked at me suspiciously, for signs of another tantrum. Then he laughed.

"Well, *Señora*, Villa de Alvarez is a small town. It is honest. Of course no one will enter."

Before he could say more a truck slammed to a halt outside the house. Two men staggered in under a big metal door. They set it in place at the street entrance.

"*La puerta!*" Nicasio cried in triumph. "Your house is now complete, almost, that is." He handed Bill a big front door key. "*Bienvenido a su casa!*" He loped off towards his *consultorio* where patients waited.

For some time we were not lonely. We had the electrician, the plumber, the carpenter, the window glass man, and the *maestro* for daily company.

At the next Wednesday gathering Gonzalo and Mari Lu arrived early. They looked our place over carefully.

"It's very nice," Gonzalo said. "Very big, very tranquil, very cheap."

"Nicasio and Ilse did it after all." Mari Lu giggled.

"Did what? What do you mean 'after all'?" I asked. "Weren't they planning to finish it?"

"Of course they were," Gonzalo said. He handed over a box with a small lemon tree which he had brought as a housewarming present. "They were always planning to. There is just one trouble with Nicasio and Ilse. We didn't like to tell you before."

"They can never finish anything," Mari Lu chimed in, laughing loudly. She pointed in quick succession at an empty space where a window should be, at the not-quite-finished tile floor, at the unfilled openings for base plugs. "Never... never can they finish anything. We would not have believed it possible that you could live in this house. But for you they nearly finished it."

"They have been building the house for eight years," Gonzalo explained, glancing out at the patio with its broken wall. "That's why the place looks a little old. We were all sure it would never be done. Of course we didn't like to tell you. Now it is you, the Americans, who have made Nicasio finish it at last, almost."

In Honor of San Felipe

"Here you will find it to your taste," Nicasio had remarked the day we moved in. "Very tranquil, just what you need. Why live in the city of Colima when you can enjoy a quiet life in little Villa de Alvarez?"

Quiet it was not. Other noises were dominated by roosters for sheer staying power. In most country places, it seems to me, roosters start crowing to herald the dawn. In Villa de Alvarez they start at eleven the night before and keep it up. Then once in a while there is the unearthly braying of a burro. Noises different from those of our Colima cottage but just as penetrating.

In Villa de Alvarez the shoeshine boy yells, the newspaper man bellows, trucks going early to the sugarcane fields change gears just beneath the bedroom window.

There are meaningful sounds. A bicycle rider tolling a cowbell means the garbage truck is coming. A tinkling rendition of White Christmas signifies ice cream cones; another ditty, soft drinks; another, the weekly fresh fish man.

There must be more holidays celebrated in La Villa than anywhere else in Mexico, judging by the barrage of fireworks. It is ten days for Saint Francis; twelve days for Guadalupe; a good three or four weeks for Christmas and New Years.

Trains passing through from Guadalajara to Manzanillo enjoy a huge opportunity, at 4:00 a.m., to awaken all citizens of both Colima and Villa de Alvarez, with prolonged, pointless whistling. The rhythm that to us means "shave and a haircut, two bits," has a dirty meaning in Mexico. The night train man once scandalized our town with a continuous rendition of this as he passed on his way to the Pacific. The town ladies buzzed about it for days.

The noise I find most pleasing is that of horses trotting or stolidly walking along our street, their riders headed for outlying ranches, the plaza, or a friend's house. The horse has not gone out of fashion in Villa de Alvarez, even though cars, trucks and motorcycles have joined the traffic.

Bill and I have lived here for several months now, but we are still a novelty. We do not get the frontal approach, as we did our first morning when we woke to find several friendly faces at the bedroom window.

"Did you sleep well? Is Villa de Alvarez to your taste?" a spokesman politely inquired. We settled this problem quickly with curtains, but there was still the doorbell.

In the evening at playtime, which here is any time up to midnight, it is always fun to ring the doorbell. For one thing, it is the only doorbell around. For another, the dog will bark. I quickly stopped answering the bell because there was never anyone there. Obviously this ringing is really done by a ghost.

Taking out the garbage is a rite which, each morning, gives the neighborhood children a chance to gawk at Bill or me.

"Here comes *Don Guillermo*. Hurry up! You'll miss it. Oh, HERE COMES THE DOG!"

Sometimes I hear a rapping at the window.

"*Doña Celia, Doña Celia, hay pomo?*"

This is Lupita, a wistful child of nine with big round black eyes and long wispy dark hair. She is dressed in a sombre brown dress, too small, which will soon be handed down to a younger sister. But she has a frayed shocking-pink shawl draped around her skinny shoulders, to liven the impression. She is a worthy recipient for a *pomo*. Since that word is not in my dictionary, I invite Lupita in to show me what a *pomo* would be if I had one: any empty glass jar.

Later I ask Lupita what she has done with the dozens of *pomos* I have given over many weeks? She answers my question with the universal statement, "*Aie*," as she bobs out of sight behind the Pepsi-Cola sign which fronts her family's shack.

From the corral behind our house comes the neighing of horses, so close they seem to be right beside the sink while I wash the lunch dishes. The nine-day-long *Feria* of Villa de Alvarez is about to begin on February 5th, day of San Felipe de Jesús. Nicasio's son Arturo and his friends have brought in the horses from the family ranch for the parade. Arturo is away in Mexico City most of the time, studying veterinary medicine, but all Villa de Alvarez citizens plan to be home for the fiesta even if they must return from far parts.

"There will be a fine parade," the *maestro* who is painting the front of our house tells us. "Much noise at night. Nine nights. Nine whole nights!" He twirls his brush dramatically, splattering drops of white on the black gate.

The *maestro* is hardly the master his name implies. In La Villa anyone who can wield a brush or tinker with tools calls himself *maestro*, though curtains may hang crooked, and shelves slant. I note that the paint around our window frames is not exactly even, but why complain? We are just carrying out a town edict. The *Presidencia*, the town hall, has issued a notice that everyone must paint the facade of his house before February 5th or pay a fine. The result is a crazy quilt of pink, white, yellow, red, green, and purple facades, some painted meticulously, others apparently doused with a bucketful of paint-and-water mixture.

"Don't miss the parade," Lupita urges every time she goes by, "I will come for you."

Everyone with a horse plans to be in the parade. This is more people than you might imagine in a town of 10,000 population. In those narrow streets with houses built contiguously, where would there be hundreds of horses? Looking through the wide front doors, open to let in the tropical breeze, I catch the flick of a pony's tail in a patio, or hear the clatter of hoofs as a goodlooking animal is led out of a garage. Most of these horses are brought in from country ranches for the big event. Riders trot and canter by our house, converging in groups at the corner store where, without dismounting, they take a rest stop for a coke or a *Sidral* and some gossip.

This village fair has a long history, two hundred years at least, and a worthy purpose: to persuade San Felipe de Jesús to avert earthquakes and protect us from the wrath of the *Volcán de Fuego de Colima*, that smoking mountain which dominates our town. Everyone claims that the one year when the fiesta was omitted for lack of funds, back in the 1930's, there was a disastrous quake.

In earlier days, when huge haciendas dominated this ranching area, the fiesta was more elaborate. Nicasio, a student of the good old days, fills us in on details. Friendly combat was engaged in with rotten eggs and eggshells filled with ashes for ammunition. People painted their faces in various hues. Torches of *ocote* lit up the night, and confetti was showered on the women in the crowd. Clowns on stilts strode about wearing striped pants, frock coats, top hats, and heavy watches on silver chains.

From the beginning the figures known as *mojigangas* headed the parade, tall images of a man and woman leering above the crowd. I don't know when these started to be caricatures of whoever was the Colima governor of the time, and his wife, but this adds to the fun, especially when the Governor happens to be unpopular, as our present one is.

The annual temporary bullring, out at the end of our street, has always been constructed in the manner we saw this year. Saplings are tied together with *ixtle* ropes and the structure is roofed around the sides with straw mats. It is adorned with festoons, garlands, and chains made of crepe paper.

This bullring is enormous, with room not only for bulls and horses, but for kibitzers as well. There will be two conventional bull fights, but on all the other days there will be informal events where the ring is jammed with cowboys roping, jugglers juggling, musicians playing, children doing balancing acts, and drunks wandering the outskirts. On these days the bulls are not killed. Their horns are taped. Young men maneuver with capes in the ring, but it is all for fun. When the bull lies down and tries to go to sleep the crowd laughs delightedly. A row of tipsy taximen sway back and forth to the music.

It is time to go to the parade. Lupita hangs on our gate. She beckons feverishly, hurry...hurry. Bill and I set out with her to the plaza a couple of blocks away. It is already crowded with spectators from La Villa, and others from Colima come to view their country cousins. There is the usual conglomeration of sellers of Chiclets, tamales, balloons and paper cups filled from a gourd with *tusca*, a potent local drink. The church with its gold cupolas is floodlit. The benches in the plaza fill up and the crowd banks along the Colima highway. The parade started two miles away in down town Colima. It is nearing La Villa. It is reported to be at the church of San Francisco...it is only three blocks off now...it is here.

The vanguard, a crowd of young bicyclists, wheels like a flock of big birds around the square, down the street, and back around again. After them come the *mojigangas*, looming high above the crowd. Their clown's faces do bear a slight resemblance to the governor and his wife. Everybody claps and the firecrackers start to go off. Roman candles and rockets whiz by within an inch of our heads. The din is like a frontline attack.

Now come the horseback riders, dozens and dozens of them, not dressed in elaborate *charro* costumes but in their regular shirts and pants. The whole thing is for laughs. There is much prancing, bucking, curveting, and passing of the *tusca* flask. Some horses have two or three riders. Some riders are facing rear. Everybody cranes, pushes, jostles. The firecrackers make me wince. I can imagine that Sam, mercifully left at home, has taken refuge under the master's bed. Finally the parade passes, the ammunition is all used up. There remains in the air only an acrid after-battle smell of smoke.

Since nothing in Villa de Alvarez is done by halves, the parade will be repeated every day for the whole nine days.

Now is the time for mariachi bands and, often drowning them out, the latest dance music from the pavilion down the street where cockfights are held and the exhibits of a smalltown fair can also be found, from bearded lady to Ferris wheel and merry-go-round.

Sleep at our house is a sometime thing as the din continues throughout the night and throughout each night thereafter. When Sam and I take out the garbage at seven in the morning there is no lineup of children to watch us. The neighborhood has better things to do. The mariachis are just going home. They stop to offer a few strains at each corner. There is a rap-a-tap-tap of trotting horses returning to patios and garages. I hear discordant singing from somewhere, cries of "*Aie*" from somewhere else.

Nine days is a long long time to keep on being merry, but in Villa de Alvarez they manage it.. And it is worth while because this year, again, San Felipe has been honored, the volcano placated. We can all sleep easy on the tenth night. This year there will be no earthquake.

Water

"It's getting very dry," Bill said one day in January. He pointed to the hillsides below the volcano. They had turned the tawny brown of ginger cookies. I had already noticed that the three rivers of Colima which I crossed on my way to the market had slowed to a dribble. Smoke floated straight upwards from the volcano into an empty pale blue sky. Hot black cinders from burning sugar fields blew through the house settling thick on chairs and tables.

In February Nicasio came to show us the mysteries of the *pozo* (the well), the *bomba* (the pump), the *tinaco* (the roof tank) and the *pilas* (the house reservoirs).

"I would have come before," he said, "but my projects have been too many. *Muy ocupado.* And anyway there is always plenty of water even in the dry season."

He turned on a faucet from which no water flowed.

"Well, maybe no water today but certainly tomorrow." We followed him to the *pozo*, the deep well back in the old horse corral. The *bomba* sat on top of the well. It was a small electric motor for sending water through a long pipe across the corral and up to the *tinaco*, or tank, on the roof for dispersal down to the bathroom and kitchen.

He handed me a gift, a beautiful pre-Columbian "Colima dog" of pottery.

"Genuine," he said. "I dug it up many years ago, when I was in medical school. I always excavated, over there towards the volcano, in the summer months. Now, at weekends, when I am not too busy, I invent."

"What do you invent?" Bill asked, while I got out the pitcher of cold *agua fresca,* a lemonady drink we kept on hand, and offered a glass.

"I am busy inventing all the time. May I have one of those cookies, please? They look delicious. *Muy sabroso.* I am at this moment working on an *aparato* that will fill *pilas* automatically, ringing a large gong when they are full."

Nicasio accepted a refill of *agua* and we all went to the inside patio to relax.

"What's that for, Nicasio? I've been wondering." I pointed to a round hole in the eaves of the covered gallery. In the rainy weeks a waterfall had gushed through it from the flat roof to flood the patio below. Now a bougainvillea soared through it skyward.

"So many projects," Nicasio murmured modestly, "and so little time. There will be a Grecian column, Corinthian style, hollow, to accept the rain water, and a drain below to carry it away. Useful. Also very elegant and decorative." He set down his glass and got up to leave.

"After all, I am a busy doctor. I did, however, finish the *pila* drain."

"Yes," Bill said, "It serves."

As usual with Nicasio, the *pila* drain was ingenious. It received the water from the *pilas* when we emptied them for cleaning. A plug at one end of the tank could be removed with a hammer. Water then gushed out in a flood into the back yard where it doubled around and over anything in its way to reach a drainpipe which led it under the kitchen floor and out again into the central patio. Here it tore along a small open trench into another pipe under the entrance hall, finally disgorging into the street to create a temporary pond at the corner store. The drain gave our *bufo* a nice place to stay.

The *bufo* is a frog- or toad-creature the size of an adolescent rabbit. In my dictionary *"bufo"* is translated as clown or joker. We saw him sometimes at night, squatting stolidly on the lawn in the moonlight. Once or twice I met him stumbling around the kitchen. The only time he appeared in daylight was when we emptied the *pila* and a torrent rushed through his living quarters. His head seemed to fill the pipe as he stared reproachfully out onto a wet wet world.

Meantime we stared reproachfully onto a dry world where *bombas* wouldn't work, *tinacos* were empty, *pozos* ran low in water, and the *Fontanero* spent an undue amount of time in the *cantina*.

March...April...May. No rain. No rain. Water became a big topic of conversation on our street, though the exchange was simple.

"Hay agua en su casa?"

"No hay."

"When *will* there be water in our house?" I asked Lupita, my small neighbor.

"On the fifteenth of June. That's when."

Not the fourteenth. Not the sixteenth. My kitchen calendar named June 15th as Santa Crescencia day. A rain goddess?

In early June dark cloud formations soared over the volcano, wind swept in from the Pacific in the afternoons. A distant rumbling could sometimes be heard. Palm leaves rattled in the gusts. The *bufo*, surly and depressed, occasionally scouted the lawn outside his pipe.

Sam, keen to the nightmare world of lightning, snuffed the air and looked skyward in the evenings. His ears went up, he whined and made for the master's bed, a sign that something dire was in the offing. The afternoon rumblings, coming from Manzanillo-way, increased. Still no rain. The Colima rivers were dry beds with hardly a memory of moisture. On June 14th the air hung heavy.

"Of course it's only a superstition," I said to Bill, "this business of an exact date for the rains to start. Who was Santa Crescencia anyway?" The day passed uneventfully except that the *Fontanero* doled out less water than usual.

"Today is June 15th," Bill said as soon as we woke up. "Time for Lupita's rain."

That day, in the afternoon, clouds banked, the volcano belched steam, gusts of wind brought the smell of ocean, palm fronds strained noisily at their stems. Suddenly, very suddenly, the deluge hit. We hurried into the house, slammed shut the windows, stuffed rags under the doors, prepared for the fury of the heavens. The *Fontanero* upstairs had finally turned on the tap.

Six tiles fell down by the kitchen door. Streaks of lightning threatened a direct hit. The din of thunder sent Sam, whining and shaking, to the bed. We set buckets below two roof leaks. Niagara rushed through Nicasio's unfinished Grecian drainage column in the patio.

Soon after the storm was over, Nicasio appeared.

"Did I not promise plenty of water?" he asked cheerfully. *"Como no."* He stopped in the kitchen for a piece of cake. *"Muy sabroso."*

We went outside to count the roof tiles which had fallen into the patio and yard.

"Next year," Nicasio told us, "I will be ready to install my new design, a *bomba-tinaco* combination such as has never been seen, although it is much needed in dry weather. Meanwhile, here is a little gift for the house.

He opened the shopping bag he carried and handed me an elegant, genuine pre-Columbian ceramic jaguar.

"I personally excavated it in the year 1955," he said, "up on the volcano. Sometime I will show you the spot."

We keep the clay jaguar on the bookcase. Its head is hollowed out. In bygone times it must have been a container for some liquid - water perhaps, or sacrificial blood. I have often studied the hideous expression on our jaguar's face, but I cannot interpret that any more than I could read the mind of our *bufo*. I think, however, that perhaps it is a smile.

El Carmen

The *Volcán de Fuego de Colima* is always capped with a swirl of steam. Sometimes in winter it is lightly filmed with snow. Experts come there to study strange reptiles or rare hummingbirds.

Our friend Dean, an expert on photographing big game in Alaska, came down to visit us. He planned to stalk the elusive *onza*, fabled cross of puma and jaguar, but when the time came we could find no one to guide us to the animal's lairs. Did the *onza* exist? We never found out for sure.

We looked for other excitement to offer our friend after his long trip. The restaurants quickly sated us with shrimps in garlic sauce. The local movie featured Shirley Temple in *Heidi.* Dean was not old enough to sit happily under a palm tree for very long.

There is one tourist attraction for which Colima is especially noted. It is not the handsome rose gardens in the plazas, or the big cathedral, or the museum of pre-Columbian artifacts, or the still-to-be-excavated pyramids in the corn fields nearby. It is not even the steaming teakettle of a volcano,

It is a collection of old American cars. Señor Zaragoza, who owns an auto parts store, has devoted years of his life and lots of money to buying and stabling all the antique Reos, Stutzes, Oldsmobiles and Packards he can lay his hands on. How they all came to Mexico, or why, is anyone's guess. I visualize a gigantic car parade crossing the border from time to time. In downtown Colima dozens of these vehicles are housed in a museum behind Señor Zaragoza's store, but the real oddity is his Hacienda El Carmen just outside the city. To reach it we took the highway which encircles Colima, then turned off onto a dirt road.

We drove the VW for a while over a narrow bumpy lane heading directly towards the volcano. Nothing unusual on the way, just a burro or two bringing baskets of corn to town, and some tiled-roof cottages under banana groves. Then suddenly, behind a high wall on the right, appeared a fairy tale castle. Disneyland transplanted to Colima! A guide appeared at the gate and for a few pesos apiece we entered to look around.

"There is no hacienda in all of Mexico like this one," the guide said, grinning and gesturing towards the turreted structure. "You will see many treasures." He pointed towards the unkempt lot which surrounded the building. Immediately I knew we had hit the jackpot in entertainment for Dean.

"I love old cars! This is great. Wow!"

He disappeared into the rusty collection of derelict jalopies that filled the yard. From time to time we heard happy cries as he came across some treasure. Bill and I stopped to examine a cage with a chattering monkey and a honeybear in it. Sam barked at the monkey, then led the way along the broad path to the castle entrance. Rustic benches, apparently made of wood, flanked the path. On closer inspection we saw that they were of knobly cement painted dirt-brown. Pseudo-wood. The wood shortage, perhaps. But the garrulous guide told a different story.

"What do you think this is?" He pointed to the ceiling as we passed through the elegant entrance hall.

"Marble, of course."

"Not so. It's wood painted like marble. Well done, don't you think? You wouldn't have guessed that it was wood, eh?"

In the chapel, stone imitated cement, while in the big sala, cement paraded as stone. Nothing in this restoration of a hacienda was what it seemed. All was illusion. An expensive illusion. In many cases to have used the real thing would have been cheaper, I expect. Ah, but that would be commonplace, wouldn't it? It would lack the spectacular touch. I wondered if Sr. Zaragoza was related to Ilsa and her guess-what cuisine.

Just as we were remarking on this, Sr. Zaragoza himself burst through the front door in a frenzy of energy. He was a large, ebullient man of fifty or so, the epitome of a successful car salesman. His tiny Señora trailed behind him in her high-heeled sandals and tight purple dress. We shook hands all around and Sr. Zaragoza welcomed us to his museum. He had just made a wonderful find up in Durango; it was on its way down to the collection. He clapped our guide on the back as he described it to him: a steam roller, American, very old, beautiful! How beautiful!

"I keep adding to my collection," he cried, turning our way. "The greatest in the world!" His short black mustache quivered with excitement.

His hacienda, we quickly gathered, was its own reason for being, needed no justification.

"Twenty years of my life well spent," he summed it up. "Very soon my wife and I are going to move out here from Colima to live. I planned all the restoration myself. Unique! I shall enjoy living here with my treasures. Would you like to take a picture of me and my wife in that Buick over there?"

Bill obliged and Sr. Zaragoza bustled off again murmuring, "Twenty years of my life well spent."

A look at Señora Zaragoza's face showed that she was not of the same opinion. She lingered behind her tornado of a husband to sit down on a marble-cement bench and rest her feet.

"I've raised seventeen children and now this," she told us, "and now this — to live here," waving an arm towards an early Ford snuggled against a dilapidated hearse. She leaped up quickly at the blare of a car horn outside, and hurried away. A flight of swallows swooped in her wake. I noticed that they had nested among the beams and the walls were thickly encrusted with droppings.

We moved along with Dean, who had now joined us, and Sam, into the center of El Carmen. This really is an ancient hacienda, four hundred years old, originally the property of Spaniards named de la Madrid. Here stone is stone and brick is brick. Arcaded passageways surround a handsome central patio with a fountain. Automobiles cram the entire space: a DeVaux with a rosebush leaning into the driver's seat, a Reo smothered in bougainvillea, a Stutz whose rumble seat houses a nest of mice. A score of other cars of ancient vintage shoulder each other around the fountain and under the arcades. Dean keeps busy peering under hoods. From his cries, I am sure he has discovered at least a couple of *onzas*. Sam loves to go for a ride. With his usual aristocratic taste he selects a custom-built Packard, leaps through the broken door into the back seat, and whines for action.

The guide now opens room after room of "restoration" surrounding the beautiful original patio. Here wood simulates cement, cement simulates marble, marble pretends to be brick, and bricks are made to look just like wood. A loving project evidently, such as, I expect, no one else in the world would have imagined, let alone have spent huge sums of money on it.

Other treasures are stacked in various rooms on different levels: ponderous typewriters, ancient flatirons, Victrolas from the era of His Master's Voice, a player piano. We lose our way in a hodge-podge of canopied beds, huge armchairs with stuffing hanging out, carved chests, a sedan chair. Dim oil paintings of dead ducks and pretty nymphs by mountain streams hang against walls gray with dust.

The roof of the hacienda is huge, open, flat. From a viewing balcony on one side we look over and down to an oval green pool, too big for a bathtub, too small for swimming. A special wall provides a peephole for viewing the volcano, which can be viewed, however, very well from anywhere on the roof, along with a sweeping panorama of mountain, valley, lemon orchards, cane fields, pastures dotted with horses and cows. The guide tells us that the young people from the neighborhood dance here on Christmas and New Years. On a moonlight night it must be wonderful.

Our tour of El Carmen over, the guide leads us down again to the old patio.

"Wait a minute," he says. "You must hear something."

He is taking advantage of what are probably his first tourists that week to give us the full treatment. Scurrying into the somber hall where nymphs and dead ducks line the walls, he unlocks a cupboard and then a box within the cupboard, and from this box takes a key. Reverently he unlocks the player piano and adjusts a roll.

"It works. Listen. It still works very well." He nods his head with satisfaction and cautiously starts the music.

We leave the fairyland castle to the tinkling strains of "Tea for two and two for tea, Just me for you and you for me" ...and are back in the real world of Mexico again.

Teacher's Day

"Are you American? Are you American?" someone called in Spanish.

I had just paid the telephone bill and was walking down to the main square in Colima. Turning, I saw a young Mexican woman, handsome and smartly dressed, hurrying across the street towards me.

She arrived panting, as I admitted, warily, that I was American.

"Will you teach me English?" She grabbed my arm. "You do live here in Colima, don't you? I've seen you before. Excuse me that I don't speak English to you now, but I so much want to learn."

"Yes," I said, "but I am not a teacher, and besides I don't want to teach."

"But you have to." She pushed back her long black hair with an impatient gesture. "Our teacher does not have the right accent." She was now practically wailing. "I'm Elena. There's Ines, Pedro, and Aquilino too. We all want to learn English the right way, but we don't know any Americans. I have studied a long time, but my English is so bad I can't let you hear it, not until you will teach us. You will, *verdad?*"

We talked for a while and I continued to refuse. Finally, in order to escape, I took Elena's address and said that I would drop in at her house next day to talk about it some more. In Colima appointments never mean much. One may or may not show up at the doctor's or the lawyer's or a friend's house. No one resents this or thinks it unusual. Taking a tip from this custom I did not keep the next day's appointment but put the whole thing from my mind. I didn't run into Elena again on the street.

However, several weeks later the doorbell rang at our house and Elena stood there. She looked tall, thin and chic in a pink cotton dress, pink pumps, her black hair flowing smoothly over her shoulders.

"Do you remember me?" she asked. "May I come in? I saw you and followed you to your house."

We settled in the living room for a cup of coffee and a chat.

"We still want you to teach us English. We have just fired our Mexican teacher. Now you must teach us. *Verdad?*" She smiled hopefully.

How did she know whether I could teach, I wondered. Had she jumped to this conclusion for some mysterious reason when she first saw me walking down the street? No, it was probably just that there were no other foreigners around.

"We know, all of us, that you will be a fine teacher," she said. "After all, it is your language, *verdad?*"

Her persistence was flattering. I finally agreed.

I thus became involved on two evenings a week with Elena, Ines, Pedro and Aquilino.

"We have a language book already," Elena told me when I agreed to teach.

"A book? That's good." I pictured a simple little grammar-conversation paperback.

"Not just one book," she explained. "Six books and we are on book four. That does not count exercise books, six of them, or separate teacher's manuals, six also. We have eighteen books altogether. They are by 'Lado', the best for English, but not easy."

"How advanced are you?" I asked in English.

She hesitated a moment, nonplused. I repeated the question in Spanish.

"We have been studying for two years," she said, "but we don't know much. That is why I am talking to you only in my language."

Our lessons were held in Pedro's office in the Edificio Cuauhtémoc, Colima's tallest (four floors) and newest office building, so new, in fact, that it was only just starting to crumble. Pedro was an accountant, a friendly, nervous fellow. He was stocky, good-looking, thirty years old or so, only happy in a hum of activity with phones ringing, typewriters clattering.

He had crowded his small office with an unbelievable assortment of memorabilia. On shelves, desk-tops, windowsills lay collections of pipes, statuettes of famous Mexicans, key rings, ash trays, match box covers, many of them from far countries.

"I have traveled a little only," Pedro explained, "but my friends and business clients have helped with my collections."

Many kinds of cactus sprang up in little pots hung on the wall or perched in corners. A ceiling fan whirled, with a soft creaking sound. Several imposing computers were lined up on a counter. Six girls practiced on the machines so that they could become Auxiliary Accountants, that is, bookkeepers. On my first visit they all looked up at me and smiled. Pedro dismissed the girls. Elena and Ines arrived. We got down to business.

Elena wanted grammar.

"How I learn use subjunctive?" she inquired wistfully, showing no interest in anything between the simple present and that recondite form. Past, future, imperfect, aroused no enthusiasm. I had vague memories of long-ago high school grammar lessons...parts of speech...tenses. Definitely, I was not cut out for this job.

"It's hard to explain, Elena," I said, "but I can give you an example. 'I wish I *were* a better English teacher.' "

"You very good teacher," she said kindly. "I wish I *were* to speak English more better. Correct, *verdad?*"

Pedro wanted to talk, in any language, as nonstop as possible. His English was somewhat overelaborated: "I can to be able must to do..." was the sort of beginning which led to a tenacious struggle towards, but seldom reaching the meaning he wanted to convey. A sentence went on indefinitely unless he was stopped. It was not easy to stop him, but the whole class was eager to help.

"Now I speak always with you English," Elena told me, as we walked together towards our cars after the first lesson. "That Pedro, I do not think I can to stand him pretty much longer."

Aquilino, although he paid for lessons, was notable by his absence. He represented a cigarette company and roamed far afield in his station wagon, filling orders for Raleighs and Kents. He usually attended classes in absentia from Barra de Navidad, Puerto Vallarta, or Ciudad Guzmán.

Ines, a demure little soul with a ready giggle, used an important English word, "Yes," which she gently inflected as a question. "We can to stoody ..yes?...little more and then we talk very quick...yes?...more better?"

Elena, the bossy one, belonged to one of the richest families in

Colima (buses, trucks, textiles), but in her late thirties she remained unmarried. She led a comfortable, apparently contented life in a big old house where she was surrounded by family: mother, father, sisters, brothers, nieces, nephews, maids, dogs. On vacations it was routine for all of them to go to the beach at Manzanillo, reserving sixteen rooms at the super-deluxe Las Hadas Hotel for a week or two.

As the lessons went on my class made some progress. They stopped telling me they walk-ed and talk-ed, and learned to say they walkt and talkt. They had been speaking, they readily admitted, real *pocho* , a derisive Mexican term for those who speak English with a heavy Mexican accent, a sort of below-the-border Pidgin. Although I never ran into him, I understood that their former teacher still held forth upstairs in the Edificio Cuauhtémoc, teaching a new group to say, "I walk-ed to the letter office where I mail-ed a letter and I can to expect maybe an answer more soon."

I struggled to become a teacher. How could I make clear that we say "I can do something," or "I am able to do something," but not "I can to do it" or "I am able do it"? Lada, the eighteen-book marvel, did little to enlighten me.

The girls were especially eager to learn about things American, for they dreamed of traveling in the United States.

"Is it true that girls in your country, when they grow up, can leave home, go to another city, rent an apartment even, take a job with strangers? Or is that just in the movies?" Ines asked one evening, using Spanish to get her meaning easily across.

When I said that this was true she explained that she could never go alone to the United States or even to Guadalajara. Her father would not permit it.

"Ines," I said, "you're twenty-four. You have an office job here in Colima. Lots of girls in Mexico City are independent, you know, just like American girls. Why don't you save your own money and travel?"

She burst into the giggle which always preceded her attempts at English. Then she frowned.

"Oh no, this is Colima, old Mexico town. I cannot never to go nowhere...yes?...My father is old Mexican. Here if woman has eighty years old and still live in home...yes? ...of Papa, she cannot to do what she wish. Must to ask him."

Elena assured me that her life was not easy either, like in the movies. She would never be allowed to take a trip alone, and yet how much she would like to see New York.

Pedro, who of course could do what he wanted, planned a Christmas visit to his aunt in San Diego, at which time he expected to speak perfect English.

"I can to be able then perhaps if hard study learn speak more little, or little more perhaps, and not so much the laughter of my cousins?"

"Yes, Pedro," I said, "maybe."

Our twice-weekly sessions continued pleasantly. Vocabularies improved but English syntax remained unaltered. Sometime before I first met my pupils they had become linguists of a surrealist type, with grammar so atrocious that I could not tell where to start correction, yet the whole effect was understandable.

So we went on for several months until the arrival of Teacher's Day. This took me by surprise. Mother's Day, Father's Day, yes. But Teacher's Day? In Mexico every dog has his day. There is student's day, doctor's day, nurse's day, postman's day, policeman's day, to name a few. There may be a day for left-handed seamstresses and one for delivery boys with three-speed bikes. Mexico's official Teacher's Day leaped at me from the calendar when I arrived at class one Tuesday evening.

We held this class, because it was a celebration, in Elena's home, a sprawling old mansion down between the bus terminal and the big market. Little of the outside world could penetrate. We sat in the fragrant patio at a graceful, carved white table, perhaps from Paris, with a frilly lamp upon it. Overhead towered an enormous sky-high mango tree from which fruit drooped close to our mouths. From the *sala* indoors we could hear two of Elena's sisters practicing duets on the grand piano. The moon rose slowly over a sloping jasmine-covered roof.

"Happy Teacher's Day!" Elena hugged me. Ines clapped her hands and cried, "Happy Teacher's Day...yes?"

No six-book studies on this day; no blackboard; no busy note-taking. The patio table was decorated with Pedro's collection of statuettes. In the center sat a big cake baked by Elena. Ines offered chocolates. Even Aquilino, hovering on his business trip from Tecomán to Atenquique, stayed long enough to smoke a Raleigh and to pour the sparkling wine. We toasted each other, Mexico, the United States, Colima, little Villa de Alvarez.

When it came time to go home, Pedro pressed flowers into my arms while Elena and Ines presented me with a huge toy animal.

They all then sang a very strange version of "Auld Lang Syne." Ines' clear soprano voice rose above the rest: "Can old a-quaintance to be forgot...yes?...And not never brought to mind..."

As I staggered to my car under the burden of presents, I realized that I was now, at last, a *maestra* in good standing, on an equal level with the "master" carpenters of Colima who nail up crooked shelves, and the electricians whose wiring short-circuits.

Maybe my class was not learning perfect English, but I had the visible symbols of success: an armload of carnations and a big stuffed rabbit.

The Day the Onza Spilled the Beans

We settled into the small town of Villa de Alvarez and so did Sam. We thought of taking him up on the slopes of the volcano to explore and follow his profession of pointing pheasants, but there were no pheasants near Colima and besides we were afraid of losing him in wild country. We might have taken him hunting for the elusive *onza* but did that animal really exist? We were never sure. Some of our neighbors claimed to have seen the big beasts, a cross between jaguar and puma, native, they assured us, only to the Volcano. There were rumors of *onza* skins on hunters' walls. We never saw the skin or any other part of an *onza*.

Meanwhile Sam appeared to enjoy village life, walking sedately on his leash to the plaza and back, stepping proudly among hounds of lesser breed. He attracted more attention than we did.

"Qué perro grande! Cómo se llama? Es bravo?"

A big dog. What's his name? Does he bite?

These questions were easily answered. Big Sam does not bite. And the neighbors soon took him for granted. But still his fame spread rapidly around Villa de Alvarez and over into Colima. We began to receive offers of mating with everything from fox terriers to Dalmatians. It was hard to explain that just because a bitch had black spots on a white background she was not necessarily worthy

of matrimony with our purebred German shorthaired pointer. Sam
had fathered a fine litter of pedigreed puppies back in Berkeley and
that should suffice.

Then one day I answered a knock on the door to find a young
man standing there.

"Buenos días, Señora," he said politely, "I am Ricardo Lopez and
way over on the other side of Colima I have heard of your fine dog
Sam. I have come to ask if I can mate him with my bitch Anka." He
gestured to a pickup truck where a dog stood watching us with
interest. I was surprised to see that she was a shorthaired pointer,
with perhaps just a soupçon of something else.

"Anka here is ready for mating," Ricardo said eagerly.

I invited him in and consulted with Bill. We agreed on the
match and arranged for Anka to drop by our place in a day or two.

I asked Pedro, one of my English students, to come over too
since I knew that while he was an accountant he would rather have
been a vet.

Anka arrived with Ricardo and we introduced the two dogs.
We were disappointed to find that there was no gesture of affection
between them. Nothing but snarling and snapping. Neither of them
seemed enamoured and Sam had even lost his know-how of the
mating process. Pedro and Bill tried to help but no go. You would
have thought that he had never been in this social situation before.

"You've got it wrong, Sam," Bill cried as he and Pedro wrestled
with the pair. "Not the ear, Sam, the other end."

Finally we gave up and told Ricardo we were sorry. He drove
away with Anka and we thought the episode over. We were surprised when he turned up again next morning with Anka and a vet,
Dr. Romero.

"I hear you're having some trouble," Dr. Romero said. "We'll
soon fix that." He flourished a large syringe. "I'll just give your dog
-Sam is it? - this little injection. Then wait three days, the bitch is not
quite ready yet, and get them together again. *Buena suerte,* good
luck."

He left and we agreed to wait three days and then take Sam to
the corral behind Amalia's store at the corner, where Anka would
be waiting. "Amalia's my cousin," Ricardo told us. "She'll be glad

to take care of the matter. I've promised her a pup."

The time of waiting was uneasy. At night Sam roamed the house restlessly, whining and yelping. In the daytime he slept, exhausted. We started out early on the morning of the third day since he seemed as ready as he would ever be. Straining at the leash he hurried Bill along the street by the postoffice, apparently sure of where he was going. A burro and three children bounded out of our way as we barreled along with Sam in the lead. Chickens squawked and the postmaster came out to look. Sam made a sharp right turn at the end of the street, dragging Bill behind him while I brought up the rear.

"*El perro grande,*" little Lupita cried as we passed her yard. "*El perro bravo! Aquí viene Sam!*"

I knew Amalia's store well. It opened on the street, occupying a corner. Behind it was Amalia's house, an imposing building of two stories built around three sides of an inside patio. There was a covered gallery with stairs up to the second floor. An iron gate led to the big corral behind the patio.

Bill entered the patio by a house door, separate from the store, with Sam pulling vigorously ahead. I followed. The patio was not empty. We were moving fast but in passing I had time to notice an old woman lying in a hammock reading a newspaper, a teenage boy over in the corner working on a bicycle, a cluster of chickens puttering about and a big goat nibbling grass.

Sam knew the approach to take. He rushed over to the corral.

Bill opened the gate, then quickly tossed me the leash.

"You take him," he said. "I'll go find Ricardo. Be careful now, don't let him go!" He hurried off to the store.

I had a quick glimpse of the corral, a big lot with several palm trees, a vegetable plot, an open stable with two horses in it, and a cow grazing contentedly on the greensward. We hesitated a moment, then Sam gave a mighty tug. I tripped and fell flat, letting go the lead. He tore into the corral.

Scrambling up I looked around for Sam. He had spotted Anka tied to a papaya tree and was headed toward her. Just at that moment she broke loose - the rope tying her must have been frayed - and took off around the corral with Sam in pursuit.

Then things happened rapidly. Anka ran round the corral twice with Sam at her heels. The cow lumbered off to a far corner and the horses neighed and stamped in their stalls. I sprang forward to shut the gate but I was too slow. Both dogs rushed through and into the patio, with Sam behind but closing. Anka, sprinting along, turned her head to give him a coquettish glance. They circled the patio once, scattering the hens. The boy stopped mending his bicycle to watch and Grandma rolled out of her hammock. After circling twice more they disappeared up the gallery stairs to the second floor balcony where they could be heard banging into things.

"*Ayeh! Qué pasó?*" Grandma cried, looking under the hammock for her glasses. A flower pot tumbled from the balcony and crashed beside her.

"*Qué perro bravo!*" yelled the bicycle boy.

"Sam," I called, "*Ven acá! Ven acá!* Come here!"

Sam ignored me. Now the dogs were down in the patio again. (It takes a while to describe these events but really they only lasted a few minutes.) I made a grab for Sam's leash as he passed me but missed it.

Now suddenly they changed course and ran straight for the store. The back door was open and they disappeared inside. Loud cries could be heard. I hurried over to see what had happened.

Amalia's store was full of shoppers dropping by to collect the morning's fresh rolls. Anka, closely followed by Sam, leaped over the counter and landed in the midst of the purchasers.

"*Cuidado! Un perro bravo!*"

"*Cuidado,* look out!" A girl pulled her little sister out of the way.

A heavily pregnant woman gathered her apron about her and retreated to a corner where she collapsed on a crate of lettuce.

"*Ayeh,*" she cried. "I have a pain. *Socorro!* Help me! Help me, someone. I have a pain!"

Amalia herself, standing behind the counter where she was measuring out some sugar, stared horrified as goods toppled from the shelves.

Meanwhile Sam had almost caught up with Anka. He was only slightly delayed by a broom which had somehow become attached to his leash. It followed him like an extra tail, sweeping all before it.

The animals vanished into Amalia's *sala* where I could hear Ricardo and Bill talking. There were sounds of a struggle and a crash as something fell over. Then the men appeared each holding a dog on a leash. They passed through the store and disappeared into the patio at a run. Bill returned in a few minutes.

"They're in the corral and I locked the gate," he said. "I guess Sam knows what to do now."

We stayed at Amalia's long enough to assess the damage: a big crate of broken eggs, rolls loose on the floor, and a lot of beans. The hamper where they were stored had overturned disgorging a river of beans out into the street. We left a contribution to take care of the breakage and said goodbye to Amalia.

"I'm sorry about the whole thing, Amalia," Bill said. "*Lo siento muchísimo.*" But Amalia was not angry. She had been promised a pup.

"*Perritos* that start like that," she told us, "what *perros* they will be. They will be brave as *onzas.*"

Out on the street a small crowd gathered.

"*Qué pasó?* What happened?"

Then Bill had an inspiration.

"It was an *onza*," he said, "a great big spotted animal. It passed through Amalia's store and frightened everyone." Little Lupita, walking beside us, laughed delightedly. "An *onza*," she cried. "An *onza* whose name is Sam!"

For the next three days everything was quiet on Josefa Ortiz de

Dominguez Street. Then we brought Sam home without incident. Eventually some splendid puppies were born. Nothing more was said about that morning at Amalia's store. But I like to think that a legend may have had its start that day. Perhaps not all the spectators were close enough to know what happened. One of them might have been way over beyond the postoffice where he heard only the words "*onza* in Amalia's store" and saw the crowd. I imagine the result:

It is years later and two old men, citizens of Villa de Alvarez, are taking the sun, sitting on one of the carved benches in the main plaza.

The two friends are reminiscing as such oldtimers will. The five golden cupolas on the church shine brightly; they have just been repainted. A gaggle of youngsters play by the fountain and the ice cream man hawks his wares.

"Nothing ever changes in La Villa," one of the old men says. "I remember when they last painted the church. It was back in the summer of '75. Time passes and nothing ever changes." He opens a paper bag and tosses some crumbs to the swallows.

"I don't agree with you, *Compadre*," his friend says. "We have come a long way. Back in those days a man was hardly safe in his own house. Wild animals came down from the volcano and roamed loose in the city streets."

" Nonsense, you're dreaming."

"It was in 1975," his friend says. "I remember the year. A long time ago. That was the year the *onza* ran through Amalia's store. Did a lot of damage I can tell you."

"An *onza*? What are you talking about? There was never an *onza* in Amalia's store."

"Yes there was. I was there. It ran through the store foaming at the mouth. It was huge, covered with spots. The store was full of people. Rosita, the big one, started having her baby right then and the children were terrified."

"I never heard that. An *onza* in Amalia's store. Imagine!"

"Yes, I remember it perfectly well. It was a Sunday morning in June. The rains has just started that week but it was sunny when I went to mass. Just like today. The *onza* suddenly ran into Amalia's store from the street. It rushed through the place spilling the rolls and some cans of soup. It broke a lot of eggs and then it tipped over a basket of beans. Half the beans rolled out onto the street. Amalia was furious."

"*Verdad!* Are you sure it was an *onza*? How did it get into the store? Why did nobody shoot it?"

"I can't tell you how it got into the store; it came from the street and all of a sudden it was there. Everybody saw it. It jumped over the counter growling and it ran through the house doing terrible damage. Then it disappeared. It vanished. It was never seen again."

"Never seen again? Are you sure you really saw it? *De veras?*"

"Of course I really saw it."

"You said you were by the postoffice. How could you see it from there? Tell me that."

"Well...perhaps I didn't exactly see it but I know it was there. It was big and savage and covered with spots. It was certainly there. There's no doubt of it. After all, I saw the beans."

Can Sam Love Linda?

Sam's mating with Anka produced six fine pups. Word spread to the dog fanciers of Colima. We had noticed no German pointers in the city, but now we heard rumors of bitches ready, almost ready, sometime to be ready. Their owners pined for handsome Sam's services. It made a nice social entrée for us too.

The first candidate did not seek us out. I happened upon her when I went to consult my new dressmaker, Señora Urtiz. Daisy (or so I thought of her; it may have been spelled Spanish-fashion, Desi), a genuine German shorthaired pointer, met me at the front door, barking and wagging her tail. She had been given to the Urtiz family by a friend in Guadalajara, where pure-bred dogs are more often raised. She was still something of a pup, only a year old, and had been thoroughly spoiled by the two Urtiz children. They promoted her from the rank of dog to that of human playmate and assigned her the best armchair for resting after games.

Señora Urtiz, somberly dressed in black, was a young-appearing woman in her forties who found her burdens almost too heavy to bear. Her husband had died suddenly, leaving her with two young children to raise, and very little money. She lived in a genteel house on the tree-shaded Boulevard Galvan and searched for a way to improve her income. Trying her hand at sewing she became a passable, though melancholy seamstress.

I made several trips for fittings. The children saw Sam, since he usually went on errands with me. Soon came the familiar suggestion — puppies!

In due course Daisy was in heat. Should we invite her to our house for a visit? We had tried with Anka and I was very much against .the use of our back patio as a honeymoon lodge.

"Could we leave Sam with you here?" I asked the Señora. "You have a walled yard. He would be no trouble, and Daisy would feel at home."

Señora Urtiz drew herself up. She sighed. She became very proper. She frowned and bit her lip.

"My children are too young for that sort of goings on," she said. "It must be at your house."

Roberto was twelve, Maria Luisa ten. I had the feeling it was about time for them to learn. However, *ni modo,* Señora Urtiz was adamant. Daisy came to our house with her feed bowl, her water bowl, her leash, and her piquant personality. She went overboard for Sam and he went overboard for his new mate. When our friend Pedro stopped by to assist he had nothing important to do. The dogs were already locked in their embrace. After three days of love-making Daisy went home.

From time to time I picked up new dresses at Señora Urtiz' house. We all waited eagerly for Daisy's offspring. The children kept me posted.

"Daisy doesn't play so much. She must rest," Maria Luisa said.

"I think she is getting fatter." Roberto poked the dog's belly gently.

Pedro made a house call. He gave the dog a physical examination and delivered his diagnosis.

"Certainly she is going to have puppies. I should say eight, but possibly nine.I have always been right about these things. Call me, Señora Urtiz, if there are complications."

Eight or nine. *"Ocho!"* cried Roberto, *"Nueve!"* He and Maria Luisa did a victory dance around Daisy who reclined in her armchair. She yawned prodigiously, wagged her tail a little, then settled down to sleep.

Daisy soon sat most of every day in her chair, resting and accepting snacks from the children. She got bigger. When the sixty-three days of gestation were nearly up she had changed from a gay young bitch into a passable imitation of Queen Victoria presiding over her jubilee. Señora Urtiz promised to call us as soon as labor started.

There was no phone call, although it was time and Daisy was enormous.

Then, one morning, while I was checking the length of a new skirt in the Señora's mirror, Daisy calmly descended from her armchair. Wagging her tail vigorously she trotted outdoors to play.

She gave up her role as Queen Victoria, quickly lost weight, and returned to her puppy ways. False pregnancy.

"It was the bitch's first heat," Pedro told us, shaking his head. "That explains it. I'm never wrong about these things. I had my suspicions, of course, but I didn't want to disappoint the children."

Pedro was undiscouraged, urged us to try once more, with another dog.

"There's Linda. Her owners, Elodia and Jesús Barreto, own the big furniture store downtown on the plaza. Good friends of mine."

"Is she a real pointer?" Bill asked. "We've been offered two Dalmatians, you know." We were anxious for a pup, this time to give to Pedro, but we wanted a pure-bred dog.

"She's a pointer *Alemán* all right...but the dog does have a drawback. As a pup she was kicked in the head by a horse. Dr. Cruz operated twice...I assisted him...and she is all right now except for one thing. She can never pull in her tongue. It hangs down always full length from the side of her mouth."

"That doesn't seem to have much to do with having pups," Bill remarked, "unless the accident upset her hormone balance."

"I'm sure she's in good shape," Pedro said, "but the Barreto kids, all five of them, are worried. They say, 'How can Sam love Linda when she is ugly?' I explained that there are times when he can love her, and one of the times is now. The Barretos would like you to come to a picnic at their place in Tonila on Saturday. Bring Sam, of course."

"You can drive out with me," Pedro added, but we preferred to take our own car. Ranch parties are a popular diversion in Colima where many families own country property and go out to it every weekend. A picnic lasts all day and most of the night. Unless you enjoy a big dose of sociability it's wise to have a getaway car.

We started early by Colima time, that is about noon. Tonila, we knew, lay off the Guadalajara highway a half hour's drive away, on the slopes of the volcano, just across the border into Jalisco. In Tonila, after the heavy fragrance of the tropics, we emerged into air so pure it was a shock. Pine trees replaced palms. A cool breeze fanned us. The volcano rose directly ahead, its higher reaches bare cliffs and lava. In the mountain town of Tonila a fiesta was in progress. Barkers called their wares, a juke box blared, children yelled. We breathed a rich aroma of hot fat and chiles. We proceeded slowly up a steep cobblestone road lined with booths for the fair. In the main square we met Pedro and the Barretos. There we also picked up Elodia Barreto's brother, who was the Tonila priest, and two young nephews. We supposed this would be all. It was to be a small family party. We jounced along a dirt track farther up the mountain and parked close to a stream. Here the Barretos had built a simple, one-room house, with a big porch where we were surprised to see quite a few people, opening hampers, lighting charcoal fires in braziers, and pouring drinks into paper cups. We were soon introduced to Aunt Concha, Uncle Hipólito, Cousin this and Nephew that.

The five Barreto children, in step formation according to height, hovered close to the porch waiting for us. The tallest boy came forward.

"I am called Javier," he said. "Where is Sam?"

"Here," Bill said as Sam leaped from the car and took off around the house at a gallop.

"And where," I said, "is Linda?"

Javier frowned. "Your *perro* is very handsome," he said. "Is he *bravo*? Does he bite?"

"No," Bill assured him. "He is gentle."

The littlest girl spoke up. "Linda is not very pretty but we love her. Here she comes now."

On Sam's second circling of the house he had been joined by a spotted pointer, a thin, sad-looking dog. Her tongue hung down several inches from the left side of her mouth. It swayed back and forth as she ran. She stopped, panting. A string of saliva dripped from the pink tongue onto the grass.

"Your dog too is very pretty," I said to the littlest girl. "In her way, that is."

"I hope your *perro* can love our *perra*," she murmured, "but I am afraid he can't. Linda is ugly."

"The name Linda means pretty," I said. "Sam can love her. "

"I don't think so." She hurried onto the porch where tacos were being passed out.

Sam and Linda started another circuit of the house. The four oldest children ran after them. The littlest girl quickly jumped from the porch, stuffed her taco into her mouth, and trotted along behind.

Pedro, who had arrived after us, settled down onto a bench and opened a can of beer.

"They may not need me to help with the mating," he remarked. "Should my advice be wanted, however, here I am."

We contributed our basket of deviled eggs to the picnic. They looked scanty in view of the mob. Every five or ten minutes a car or pick-up chugged up the lane with more of the immediate family. By three o'clock, when, sated with food and beer, we rested on the grass near the porch, we counted thirty-nine close relatives. The dogs and children, however, were not in sight.

"It's perfectly safe here," Jesús Barreto said. "The children won't get lost. They know every tree and rock. They are very interested in the dogs, of course. Your handsome Sam and our Linda..." He chuckled. "We'll see. *Vamos a ver. Verdad?*"

As the sun dropped and the sides of the volcano were draped in shadow, we found it time to go home. But where was Sam? Where was Linda?

We said our goodbyes to Elodia and Jesús Barreto. Bill whistled and called, "Sam!...Sam!!" A small echo came back from the cliffs above us.

"That dog," Bill said crossly. "I'll have to get the leash and go looking for him." He turned towards the car.

Just then the Barreto children, the five of them still in formation from tallest in front to shortest bringing up the rear, emerged from the bushes. At the head of the procession Sam and Linda walked sedately beside Javier. The children hurried towards us and Javier presented Sam.

"Your *perro*," he said, "your fine *perro*, he is *muy macho*. He can love our dog."

Pedro came down from the porch, a can of beer in his hand.

"Everything will be fine with the bitch," he said, nodding gravely. He finished his beer and set the can on the porch railing. "When the time comes, I will assist. You can count on me. There will be eight or nine pups. I am always right about these things."

Now the littlest girl stepped forward, her eyes shining. She leaned over Linda and hugged her.

"Sam did not notice anything bad," she whispered to the dog, whose tongue hung out long, limp and wet. "Linda, he thought you were *bonita. Muy bonita.*" She hugged the dog again. "Sam can love Linda."

She jumped up and ran into the house for a taco, the bitch shambling slowly along behind her.

Visitors

"Friends are coming to Mexico," I told Maria. "We must sweep and dust. Everything in the house must be *bien arreglado.*"

Maria flourished her purple feather duster. Her short black hair fell over her eyes as she nodded emphatically.

"*Sí, Señora, claro.*" She flipped a spider web from a corner of the portal. "Everything will be perfect...Are they coming from California?"

"Yes, from Berkeley, where we used to live before we retired here in Villa de Alvarez." I pulled out a drawer in the bureau looking for a tablecloth. We've gotten kind of sloppy, I thought, eating off a bare kitchen table all the time. I chose a pink cloth with emerald peacocks, a gift from Elena last Christmas.

"*Qué bonito, Señora!*...How pretty!...will your friends speak English?"

"Of course. They will not speak Spanish. It is their first trip to Mexico."

"California is far away...farther than Guadalajara?" Maria

exchanged her duster for a broom and raised a storm of dust from the red tile floor of the *portal*.

"Much farther away. They will certainly not speak Spanish."

"None at all? *Qué curioso.* Doesn't everyone speak Spanish, even if it is different Spanish, like yours, Señora?" Maria suppressed a giggle.

"You mean bad Spanish," I said. "No, they won't even speak bad Spanish."

"*Qué lástima.* Too bad. I would like to hear about *Disney-landia.*"

Maria shook her head sadly. She laid aside the broom and went off to mop the kitchen floor.

I walked into the back patio to cut some roses for the guest rooms. I had thoughts that disturbed me. We only knew the Conners slightly, but acquaintances look you up if you live in an exotic place. I remembered them from two years ago in Berkeley as pretty formal people. I wondered how they would like La Villa. I hate myself for it, but I do worry about what other people think. After two years, California was far away.

Steve, Ann and nine year-old Jimmy would arrive from Mexico City on *La Guajolota,* the "hen turkey" as Colimans called it. An eighteen passenger Twin Otter belonging to *Aeronaves del Sur,* it sidled in along the flanks of the Colima volcano every morning about ten o'clock, coming from the capital via Apatzingán, Michoacan. Our airport is listed in guides as having "no navigational aids." Bush pilots and owners of private planes use it constantly, but this was the only commercial flight to touch down at Colima.

"They'll be tired," Bill said. "I don't know how the plane manages to take three hours to get here."

"We had better start for the airport early," I said. "Sometimes it comes in ahead of time."

It was a lovely spring day as we started out in the VW combi. Just that morning I had noticed with pleasure that the tall *tabachín* tree in our back patio was suddenly in full bloom — my favorite Mexican tree with its sweet smell and mass of orange-red flowers. Later in the season the long brown seed pods would rattle in the summer storms.

Two blocks from home we reached the *periférico,* the new high-way circling Colima and Villa de Alvarez. Because it was built of cobblestones, as are many new streets in the city, it looked old. It might have gone back to early Spanish days instead of just last fall. A gritty dust rose in clouds into the still air. We could smell lemons from a grove close by. In a more distant field cattle browsed. There were a few Brahma bulls, white, humpbacked and massive among them. Two skinny curs leaped out of the roadside bushes to snarl meanly at Sam, who was lording it in the back seat. In the distance, on the right, rose the mountain range between us and the Pacific. From here it looked bare and desolate, crag towering behind crag in the misty morning air.

I moved my arm from the open window. The sun was already too hot.

A flash of color. A brilliant, all-scarlet little bird flew across the road just in front of our windshield. Another, and another.

"Wonder what those birds are," Bill said. "Scarlet tanagers or something? You ought to know. You've read the bird book."

The pamphlet on birds of Colima had done me little good except that I would like to write a poem using those names: Greenish Elaenia...Social Flycatcher...Bright-rumped Attila... Blue-hooded Euphonia...Could they be real?

"I'm sure those birds are Elegant Trogons," I said.

Soon we passed by the river where the road dips down and there is a flat gravelly stretch of beach for car-washing. We lumbered over a rough spot, our ten-year-old van creaking in its joints. Two buses and a taxi, backed into the stream, sat almost hub-deep in river water as boys sloshed them down, singing more or less in unison, *"Malague...ue...ue...ña sal...e...rosa."* The taxi boy's fine falsetto soared higher and longer on *Malagueña.* He caught up with the others on *salerosa,* and slapped the car hood with his wet rag.

Along a stretch of boulevard with a center strip the *jacarandas, primaveras,* and *tabachínes* were all in bloom at once, a rainbow of purple, yellow and red. As we turned into the airport road we passed the bread man on his bicycle, outward-bound to deliver rolls and sweet cookies to neighboring homes and ranches. The enormous straw basket on his head swayed a little, as did his huge

belly, when he swung around the corner. The bread was fresh-baked; we could smell it as we passed. He raised a hand to us in salute and with the other hand snapped a fly from his nose. The bicycle wobbled.

"We tried his sweet rolls and cookies once, remember?" I said. "They're made in all shapes and sizes, with different names, but they all taste alike."

We made the ritual stop at the railroad tracks. Here the air smelled of rotting fruit and flies. No train in sight, of course. Just a lone handcar with two men in it, clattering back and forth on the tracks, 100 feet this way, jolt, 100 feet back, jolt. Some sort of game, I guess.

We turned sharply right under a canopy of palm trees (Colima likes to be called the "City of the Palms") and were almost at once at the airport, a simple concrete shack with a handful of people standing out on the strip. We parked the car and joined them.

"It is early...there it comes now." Bill pointed toward the volcano. Something about the little plane outlined against the mountain slopes reminded me of a daddy-long-legs moving along a wall, but I could see the turkey resemblance too, as it let its wheels down. It circled several times, warily, landed some way off, and scuttled over to where we waited. The engines groaned and died, sending out a billow of gas fumes. The pilot jumped down to shake hands with buddies. The copilot joined him shaking hands with other buddies. I had a feeling that congratulations were being passed, on making a safe trip once more. Luggage was tossed casually to the ground. Then the boarding ladder came out and passengers disembarked to shake hands with relatives and friends.

"Hi there. How was the trip?" Bill called as Steve came down the ladder.

"I feel as if we've been flying all day. My God, what are all those desolate, forsaken little villages up in the mountains? No roads, looks like. Do people really live there?"

Then young Jimmy jumped down the last two steps of the ladder. He had grown a few inches since I saw him last.

"I got to sit in the cockpit and talk to the pilot. Great trip." He hurried over to shake hands formally with pilot and copilot, then seized a large suitcase from the ground and staggered off with it towards the car.

Ann stepped off last. She looked smart and neat, in highheeled city shoes, linen suit, stockings.

"Frankly," she said, "I'm very happy to get here at all. I was never so scared in my life. Steve says the mountains were beautiful but I didn't look out the window. *I don't* like small planes."

"Did you have breakfast?" I took her coat and picked up the last suitcase.

"We had breakfast all right. It was serve-yourself. No stewardess, good coffee and guess what? Green jello!"

With everyone loaded aboard the combi we set out on our return trip.

"Interesting country, Mexico," Steve remarked, "fertile, but it doesn't look very developed. I guess this is one of those third world places where they could do with some of our know-how."

"They have their own kind of know-how," Bill said. "Colima is a prosperous state, and the city of Colima is one of the richest in Mexico."

"I want to climb the volcano. Hey, there's smoke coming out of it," Jimmy said. "Looks easy. Bet I could do it in a day if I had my hiking boots."

"Fortunately you don't," Ann said, "but we have been looking forward to something different and exciting. Do you know that Colima is hardly mentioned in the guidebooks, and we couldn't find Villa de Alvarez on the map at all."

"I know," I said. We were now entering Josefa Ortiz de Dominguez Street, home territory. I cringed slightly, seeing with a stranger's eye the tumbledown assortment of shacks, adobe houses with peeling paint, Pepsi-Cola signs; everything, however, mercifully shrouded in tropical foliage.

"It's all so picturesque," Ann cried. "I can't wait to explore the city."

City, I thought. Colima, yes maybe, but Villa de Alvarez...

"That's a *primavera* tree, Ann," I said, pointing urgently to the right. "And there's a *chirimoya*, the one the burro is tied to. The big one with the orange flowers is a *tabachín*."

This deflected her attention from the *jacal* on our left, a mansion some newcomers had erected with pieces of corrugated iron and cardboard cartons. I hoped their youngest child was wearing some clothes this morning, but I knew he wasn't. Funny how boy children in Mexico can go naked, girls never. Even the corner store with its cowboys outside on their horses drinking cokes, looked very seedy. Usually I liked it. It was typical *Tejana* — "Texan" — the Mexican term for Western movies. Concha, the store owner, and I were good friends. She was out in front collecting the empty coke bottles. She waved and smiled to us. Ann, looking surprised, nodded slightly and raised her hand in a gracious gesture.

"I want to ride a horse," Jimmy said. "Ask them if they can take me riding."

"You're too young, Jimmy." Ann sounded cross. "And remember, dear, those men don't even speak our language."

I pointed to local attractions: some nice pink and blue houses, the town hall, the gold-domed church towering in the background. We stopped to let a truck go by. The pungent odor of pineapples filled the air.

"And there's our house..." I gestured to the freshly painted white house with its red-tiled roof, embarrassingly palatial alongside its neighbors. Ann followed my pointing finger, then suddenly she turned to the car window and froze.

"What's THAT?"

Close beside the car stood a young fellow with a shot gun over his shoulder. In his free hand he held by the tail a very big dead iguana.

"*Quiere comprarlo, Señora?*...You want to buy it?"

"It's horrible looking." Ann gave a yelp, her face wrinkled with disgust. "Look, Steve, look at that dreadful thing."

"No," I said to the young man. "We don't want it today. Some other day perhaps."

"It's an iguana," Bill said, "like a big lizard with bumps on it. They're good eating. Taste like chicken."

"I want to eat an iguana!" Jimmy yelled. He stared back at the animal, fascinated.

"Don't worry," I told Ann. "We're not going to serve you iguana."

"Or if we do," Bill muttered, "we'll tell you it's chicken."

"And there's our house..." I gestured again. "Here we are at the Casa Wakefield. *Bienvenido.*"

Bill parked the car and our guests climbed out.

"It's nice and white." Ann surveyed the building. Like many Mexican houses, the front is unostentatious. A square-looking one-story building with overhanging roof, flush to the street. It is attached to a neighboring home on the left, while on the right is the garage which our landlord, Nicasio, has not yet finished. It is partly roofed over and will probably remain so, but the essential iron-grill gate is in place.

The recently painted facade of our house had already tempted school children to practice their homework with big black crayons. 2 + 2 = 4? was written in foot-high letters while beside it a small word, *puta*, had been added. I didn't feel discriminated against because all the house fronts had some kind of scribbled decoration, not all of it school work.

Bill unloaded the bags and unlocked the big front door. My heart rose as we opened it upon a scene that always delights me — the central patio with its surrounding arched *portal*, off which all our rooms open. Helped by the climate we had filled the whole area with plants: roses, hibiscus, gardenias in the patio itself; a purple and blue passion flower vine masking the wall towards the garage; pots of ferns, palms, geraniums, and shiny unnamed shrubs lining the colonnade.

"Why, inside it's *pretty*," Ann said. "It really is pretty."

We showed our guests to their rooms. Jimmy, attracted by the ceiling fans, was ready to spend all day pushing buttons for off, 2, 3, 4, high, 4, 3, 2, off.

"Super," he said. "When can I go out and shoot an inagua?"

Ann changed into a sun dress and sandals.

"The stuff I traveled in is filthy," she said. "Can I just stick it in the washer?"

The washer...Maria came in and I introduced her.

"This is Maria," I said, "my washing machine, and a nice girl besides." Maria gabbled a quick greeting and withdrew to the kitchen, sensing at once that there could be no heart-to-heart talk of *Disneylandia*.

"The maid's cute," Ann said, as we explored the house. "But don't you miss a freezer, a dryer, all those things?"

"I'd sort of forgotten...We've been down here quite a while, you know."

The doorbell rang. Ann and I went to open it.

"*A vender. Muy barato.* The best one, the cheapest in La Villa."

The boy who said this was very small, about the size of the live turkey he grappled with. Its feet were tied but one wing was loose and flapped violently. The child ducked each time the wing passed over his head. The bird gobbled furiously, its red wattles bobbing up and down. The little boy held his ground, dancing on the hot cobblestones in his bare feet.

"*No quiere comprar, Señora? Muy barato.* Very very cheap."

The turkey squawked.

"Not today," I said. "*Lo siento mucho.* Some other day, *chico.*"

The boy staggered off around the corner. I wouldn't put odds on bird or child. They were evenly matched.

"Nothing we need like a live turkey," I said to Ann as I closed the door. "Besides, I have an idea the owner might come around looking for it."

"Not that you'd be interested," Ann told me, "but they've got a new frozen turkey dish in the market at home. Dark and light meat, sliced, with gravy and a hunk of cranberry sauce on top. You just stick it in the oven. A few seconds in a microwave."

"Yeah?" I said. "Doesn't sound so special. Why don't they put *mole* sauce on it?"

Bill had just come in from showing Steve the corral.

"Wonderful rich land," Steve said. "It's a pity they don't make something of it. Back where I was raised..." I had forgotten that Steve grew up in Iowa.

"I'll mix you a drink," Bill said. "Then we'll have lunch and rest. Then we'll see the sights."

"I don't want lunch. I want to go down to the store and have a coke and sit on a horse." Jimmy turned the ceiling fan to "high."

"One thing at a time," Bill told him. "Better stay here. We're having iguana stew for lunch."

*****

A week passed quickly. A day at the beach, a day with a picnic on the outposts of the volcano. The old car museum, and the museum of pre-Colombian artifacts.

I'm getting a kick out of this," Ann said one evening. She sounded surprised. "Funny they don't put it in the guidebooks much. It's really not bad."

We made a trip to Comala, a beautiful little town a few miles up the hill. It used to be called "Comala the White City," with everything starkly white from the town hall to the meanest hovel, the huge plaza surrounded with shady white arcades filled with white lacy benches. The only color, beds of red roses and a fringe of green laurel trees. The townspeople were proud of their city. Picture postcards of it sold well down in Colima. Too beautiful to last. Some local doctor put out the word that, in strong sunlight, white is bad for the eyes, can even lead to blindness. The villagers were impressed. Now we saw purple shacks, arsenic-green facades, a red cantina.

Up beyond Comala the highway continues fifteen miles to San Antonio, a ghost town and abandoned hacienda 4,000 feet up in the volcano foothills. The road is well paved, much better than the main highway to Guadalajara. At San Antonio, however, it simply ends at the plaza. In the quiet dusty square pigs and goats roam. Beyond the town is a series of wooded hills and deep ravines, a roadless stretch of country uninhabited, perhaps unexplored.

"I *like* it here." Jimmy jumped out of the car as soon as Bill had parked it under the big *parota* tree by the well. "Gonna camp in the hills.Where's my sleeping bag, Mom?"

"At home," Ann said. "It's sort of lonely up here, don't you think?"

"As a matter of fact," Steve put in, "I can see developing a place like this, with the good road already in. Some summer cabins — A-frames, probably. I bet there's good hunting."

We strolled around. There is a coffee mill at San Antonio, filled with broken-down machinery ("What a waste," Steve said); there is an old aqueduct, and a heavy smell of coffee still hangs in the air. Only a caretaker lives in the beautiful ruined hacienda, which must have seen extravagant parties in the old days, when horsedrawn carriages came and went over rutted roads, and servants hurried to pour rare French wines or unpack hampers of delicacies brought in from the city. The big *sala* echoed to our footsteps, the family chapel was dark with shutters closed. In the kitchen only a huge iron pot in one corner reminded us of the activity which once went on here.

"Sort of eerie, isn't it?" Ann said. "I don't think I'd like to be up here at night." She started back to the car.

"How come they built that highway?" Steve asked. "It's a beautiful road but we didn't meet a soul on it and it stops right here. I can't see the point of it."

"There isn't any point of it." Bill's tone suggested that there were lots of things around here with no point, and who cares.

"But somebody must have built it. Cost a whale of a lot of money too. I bet the Mexican government didn't pay for that."

"Actually," Bill explained, "Petiño, the Bolivian tin king, the man who built Las Hadas Hotel in Manzanillo, planned to develop something here, maybe a hunting lodge. All he ever got around to was the road."

"A tin king, you say?" Steve looked again at the dusty plaza as we got into the combi. "Must be something to the idea. Maybe it *would* make a good resort."

"I've heard of Las Hadas Hotel," Ann put in. "It's in the guidebook."

"I've been trying to put my finger on the problem," Steve told Bill, as we drove back to La Villa. "The problem with the people, I mean. They don't seem to do much. Takes someone from Bolivia, you said yourself, to get things going."

"I don't know if I want to get things going." Bill stopped the car to let a pig across the highway. "I don't see any point in it."

*****

The Conners left Colima by bus. They had had it with the plane, and the plane had also had it. The company had just gone broke leaving Colima with no air service.

"You must come back to Berkeley," Ann told me seriously, the day they left. "You people have been down here too long. This place is way far out. It's possible to go down hill in a town like this, not that you have, of course. But you've simply got to get back to civilization. Don't you miss the city? Think of everything that goes on there."

I did think for a moment, but it seemed a long way off. Damn Ann, why should I feel guilty?

"Thanks," I said. "We'll come up for a visit soon. I suppose we must be getting stale here. Thanks for mentioning it."

"It's time to go down to the bus station." Bill swung the car keys and hummed a bar from *Cuatro Milpas* as he went out to start the combi.

"It won't be a bad trip," he told Steve, as we backed out of the garage and headed along Josefa Ortiz de Dominguez Street, past the big trees already shedding their many-colored flowers. "It's only four hours to Guadalajara and you'll catch the eight o'clock plane in the morning. You'll be home in Berkeley in time to put the frozen turkey in the oven."

Epilogue

"We've been here two years today," I said to Bill, as we parked the combi and went into the house. We had just finished seeing our guests, Ann, Steve and Jimmy Conner, off on the bus to Guadalajara.

Bill nodded. He poured himself a glass of cold *agua fresca*, picked up a book, and headed for the back patio.

"Those people made me feel sort of guilty," I said, following him out.

"Why, for God's sake? Don't you like it here?" His tone was firm.

"Of course I like it here; I always have. I guess I feel guilty because I enjoy it here, getting nothing much done." I stooped to pull a weed from the smooth grass lawn.

Bill turned to me. He yawned. "I feel especially relaxed," he said. "Honey, we planned to give ourselves two years in Mexico to think over our retirement. What have you decided?"

"Same as you," I said.

We went into the back patio. Sam picked a spot of shade near the wall under an overhanging trumpet vine. He flopped, panting a little, his hound ears spread out on the grass. His tail wagged slightly, then was still.

Bill and I moved our lounge chairs (American, lugged down from Berkeley in the combi) out of the sun and into a corner of the patio near the dog. Our tall *tabachín* tree cast afternoon shadows, and the smell of yellow roses reached me from a nearby bush. I picked one, to bring the smell closer, and sat back in my chair. The flower felt hot and damp in my hand. It wilted quickly. Bill reached over and touched my shoulder. Suddenly I felt a surge of happiness.

"I'm glad we're here in Colima," Bill said. "This is home." He lay back and thumbed the pages of a paperback mystery from the "Happy Tiger" bookstore in Guadalajara.

I felt too lazy to read. I lay looking up through interlocking branches of trees of various heights: the young pale-green guava, the lemon tree with its shiny dark leaves and small green unripe fruit, the big shady *tabachín*, loaded with orange-red flowers and, way way above me, one of our seven coconut palms. I heard a heavy thud which I identified as a coconut dropping into the corral. The old mare in her thatched stall whinnied and stamped her foot. Somewhere chickens clucked.

"I wish Nicasio would get around to having the coconuts cut," Bill said. "Sometime I suppose one will drop on us."

"I doubt it. Anyway, the old coconut cutter is dead, remember? Nicasio said he worked for sixteen years. Then one day the rope slipped and he didn't make it. Nobody younger seems to want the job."

Sam snored. A fly tickled his nose. He woke up and snapped, then yawned hugely and fell asleep again, his forepaws crossed as though in prayer. I leaned down to stroke him, admiring the smooth glossy coat, the nicely arranged spots.

"Sam is pretty old," Bill said. "Do you realize he's almost nine? That's getting along for a dog."

"I suppose it is."

I stared up through the trees to a small boat-shaped cloud sailing past the palm tree slowly, as though not quite becalmed in a wide blue sea. A lizard scuttered over the grass by my chair. I dozed.

The bells on the plaza church rang out suddenly and woke me. They rang, I supposed, to show that time passed, but certainly not how much time. The church clock had stopped at 10:40 last year.

Life in this timeless town... I felt content.

"This book isn't much good," Bill said, tossing it onto the grass. "I'll try another one tomorrow."

His eyes rested on the hole in the corral wall. It was roughly closed, as it had been when we moved in, with boards laid crosswise. "Nicasio ought to put a gate in there," he said. "It's been that way for months. I must remember to call him again. Remind me, will you?"

I nodded.

"And by the way," he mumbled, closing his eyes, "when are you going to start writing that book you're always talking about, the one on retiring in Colima?"

"Who knows," I said. "Not today, anyhow."

We fell asleep in the shade of the *tabachín* tree.

Celia Wakefield was brought up in New England. She has traveled extensively, contributing travel articles to magazines such as *Punch* and *The Atlantic*. This is her third book. *"High Cities of the Andes"* recounts her adventures in South America. *"Searching for Isabel Godin"* is the story of the first woman to go down the Amazon.